Motivate!

A Collection of
Compelling Words and
Phrases for
Senior Activities

Compiled by
Pamela Stoltman
M.S.S.W., A.D.C., C.A.L.M.

Motivate!:
A Collection of Compelling Words and Phrases
for Senior Activities

This book was produced in an autism friendly
manner. Cover and book design by Aspie
Friendly. For more information, please visit
www.AspieFriendly.org.

First Edition

ISBN-10:   1461196140
ISBN-13:   978-1461196143

Wholesaler Title ID: 3614724

For my father,
who loved words.

Contents

Preface

Throughout an Activity Professional's career, it has always been a struggle to come up with new and exciting words and expressions. Words and phrases which describe an activity that has sparkle and flair, that will engage our residents enough to encourage them to grasp life and participate.

The words and phrases we use are so important to the well-being of our seniors, and the ways in which we motivate them, that in recent years, Activity Professionals started to be audited for the words used in all written materials related to seniors and their activities. The language we use needs to paint a compelling picture of our events, so our residents are almost waiting in the halls for the ultimate boredom buster!

It can be frustrating, time consuming and flat out annoying to not be able to come up with the word or expression you want, at the moment you need it. This book was written to be a reference tool; a compilation of words and expressions to make it easier for Activity Professionals to get senior community residents up and active!

Some of these phrases are fresh and creative, and others are tried-and-true. Whatever the occasion, there is a word, phrase or catchy saying in this reference book for you to use. This book is not sorted alphabetically, but by topic, so that you can reference the words the way you are likely to need them. It is designed to not only be a tool for you to use, but to inspire you, in using your own work and projects!

Now... "Ready, set, go!"

~Pamela Stoltman
M.S.S.W, A.D.C., C.A.L.M.

Tips For Using This Collection

This collection of words is simple concept, but following a few tips will help you turn this book into a working tool that you are likely to use every day.

Break The Rule And Write In This Book!

Highlight words and phrases you love, and mark out anything you can't use for one reason or another. This is YOUR book to use as a tool! (Don't forget to put your name in it so you will get it back after colleagues want to borrow it!)

Keep Your Eye On The Seasons

Seasonal Sections have words and phrases that can be used many ways, and are good over an extended period of time. (Instead of, for instance, a specific outing.) Also, words and phrases are categorized within the season when they occur, so reading through the seasonal sections is important.

Review The Collection Before You Need It

The words and phrases in this collection are sorted, although many of the words can be used many different ways. Reviewing the book before you need it will prevent those "where did I see that?!" moments!

Find What You Need In "More Words"

The "More Words" section of the book has many words and phrases that are general, and can be used in so many different ways, that I thought it unfair to the reader to classify them! Another benefit of this section is that it contains phrases that are great for marketing your facility, such as "what's right for you, right now". Phrases like these can be used when you are working with, or writing for, potential residents or families!

Quick Reference & Matrix For Cross Reference

The Quick Reference section in the back of the book is for to write your own favorite words and phrases! Whether they are your own, or from the book, this is a great way to have your favorite compelling words at your fingertips. The At-A-Glance Matrix is a quick and easy way to see words that have many uses. What others can you find?

Lastly, Have Fun Using This Book!

Section 1

Wellness/Health/ Beauty Programs

"One way to put exciting words and phrases to good use in your newsletter is to provide health and beauty opportunities to residents, such as 'produce the style of your life with a resident fashion show', or 'come to the Comfort Zone to refresh and revitalize with a facial or hand massage'!"

~Pamela Stoltman

Section 1
Wellness/Health /
Beauty Programs

A Brand New View
A Vision Of Timeless Beauty
Achieve
Add Variety
Aged To Perfection
All Together Now
Amplify Natural Beauty
Area Of Environment
Array Of Chic
Be A Happiness Projector
Be Well
Beauty And Timeless Style
Beauty Tune-Up
Bold, Whimsical & Flirty
Break Out
Brilliant Balance
Building Independent Skills
Calming Sensation
Calming Waters
Care Of Yourself
Carefree Countdown
Challenge
Challenge Yourself
Character Builder
Cheer Factor
Classic Beauty
Clear Vision
Comfort Zone

Disarm W/ Charm
Ditch The Negative Emotions
Don't Have To Look Old Hat
Don't Stereotype Me
Dressed To Kill
Elegance
Endlessly Glamorous
Enduring Beauty
Energetic Chaos
Everyday Confidence
Everyone Is Jumping
Experience The Classic Beauty
Express Your Style
Feel Like A Star
Feel The Difference
Feeling Great!
Feeling Sluggish
Fight The Look That Really Ages You.
Flawless
Focus
Frame Of Mind
Fresh New You
Fresh Start
Fresh Vitality
Freshen Up Your.....
Fresher Thinking
Fun Factor
Future Self
Get A Leg Up
Get Happy
Get The Style You Desire
Get Your Style Back
Getting Back On Track
Getting Personal

Getting Started
Getting To Your Good Place
Giggling Infectiously
Glamour To Go
Global Glamour
Go Figure!
Graceful, Playful
Grasp Life
Have Comfort And Joy
Head To Toe
Healing Friendships
Health Benefits
Healthy Decadence
Healthy Gardner
Healthy Outdoors, A Place To Heal
Healthy You
Help Maintain Health
Hidden Assets
Hues To Your Health
Ideas For Living Well
Imagine...Wanting More And Getting It
Improve Your Smile
In The Zone
Inspired
Inspired By Life
Instant Style
Invigorate Your Senses
Invisible Beauty
It's All About You
Jumpy Vitality
Let It Go
Let's Get Moving
Life Has A Rhythm
Lighten Things Up

Lighten Up
Live A Good Life
Live The Life You Want
Live Well
Live Your Life
Lives & Breathes
Look Good ..Feel Great
Luxury...Necessity...Or Both?
Make An Appearance
Make It A Part Of Your Lifestyle
Make It Happen
Manners & Morals
Maximum Merriment
Maximum Potential
Natural Instincts
Never Miss A Laugh
No More Melt Downs
Notice The Difference
One To Move, Two To Bend, Three To Be You
Again
Open The Door To Hope
Path To Perfection
Pep Up
Personal Style
Picker-Uppers
Posture Perfect
Primetime
Quiet Elegance
Quiet Retreat
Reaching New Heights
Reason To Smile
Recycled Chic
Rediscovering
Refreshed

Relaxation Begins With Reliability
Relaxed
Renew
See The Benefits
Seeing Past The Present
Sensational Spa
Sense Of Character
Sense Of Tranquility
Serene
Set Realistic Goals
Setting New Standards
Sitting Pretty
Smooth
So Appealing
Soar To New Heights
Soft Touch
Soothing For Mind And Body
Soothing Your Style
Sophisticated
Southern Character
Spruce Up
Stand Out From The Crowd
Stand Tall
Stay Motivated
Step It Up
Steps To Style
Stretch Your Legs, Open Your Mind
Stunning Retreat
Style
Style Confection
Style Made Simple
Style Statement
Style With Out Excess
Style...With A Little Edge

Sure Shots
Taking Unnecessary Risks
The Best Movers
The Good Life
The Path To Simplicity
The Style Of Your Life
This Season Give The Gift Of Relaxation
Time Is Marching On
Timeless Classic
Timeless Elegance
Tools And Tips
Trendy
Twist & Shout
Unbeatable Style
Unclog Your Mind
Use Good Scents
Variety
Walk Yourself Thin
Weighing In
Wish To Express Ourselves
Worth Their Salt
Your Unique Style

Section 2

Food

"When you are sending an invitation to the family, for a feast served by your chef, ask them to '...grace your tables, laden with fanciful foods and a seduction of chocolate'!"

~Pamela Stoltman

Section 2
Food

A Cut Above
A Dramatic Mix
A Taste For The Extraordinary
A Winning Combination
Abundant Experience
All The Trimmings
At 1st Blush
Baking Memories
Beat The Heat With Some Frozen Treats And
Icy Cold Drinks
Breeze Out For Lunch
Bring Fireworks To The Table
Burger Boutique
Chocolate Lovers Rejoice
Colorful Flavors
Come Hungry
Cookie Forest
Culinary Classics
Dance Through Greece
Dear Taste Buds We've Been Thinking About
You
Delectable
Dinner For Two
Down Home
Eat Well To Night
Eat, Pray, Love
Edible Blooms
Enjoy This Very Singular Treat
Entice
Epicurean Knowledge

Every Taste Has A Feeling
Experience The Flavor
Explore The Taste
Fanciful Foods
Fired Up For Dinner
Flavor Your World
Food Finds
Food For Thought
For The Love Of ...Apples
Freeze Frame
French Connection
French Frills
Fresh
Fresh Picks
Fresh Start
Frosty Treats
Fruit Of Labor
Garden Fresh
Getting Saucy
Go Ahead Splurge
Going Crackers
Going Nuts
Gooey Goodness
Gourmet In A Moment
Grace Our Tables
Great Food Served With A Side Of Fun &
Relaxation
Great Greek Delights
Homemade Decisions
Hot Stuff
Indulge Your Passion For....
International Food Tour
Just A Taste
Keeping Things Spicy

Last Bite
Lip Smacking Librations
Live Well
Master Your Menu
Matters Of Taste
Easy, Local And Flavorful
Midnight Snack
Mix It Up
More Please
Mouth Watering
Natural Sweetness
No Cooking Required
On The Side
One Pot Pleasures
Potent Potions
Restaurant Survival Guide
Ripe For Discovery
Saucy & Sensational
Secrets Of The Savory
Seduction By Chocolate
Shell Seekers
Signature Drinks
Signature Taste In A Fresh New Way
Simple Pleasures
Slam Dunk
Small Indulgence That Seduces Your Senses
Smorgasbord
Snack Shack
Sophisticated Palate
Southern Comfort N' Joy
Southern Soul Bbq
Spice Of Life
Spice Up Your Life
Steady Diet Of Love

Stir Up Some Fun
Stroll Through Spain
Stylish Confections
Sumptuous
Sure Shots
Sweet & Savory
Sweet Sips Of Autumn
Sweet Spot
Sweet Summer Social
Sweet Tooth
Sweet, Salty And Southern
Ta-Da
Tailgating Time
Take A Bit
Taste
Taste Buds
Taste Of Tailgating
Taste Of The South
Taste Of Tradition
Tasty Twist
Tempting Treats
Terrific Taste
The Foodies
The Perfect Blend
Thirst Quenchers
This Should Be Interesting
Time For Tea
To Dine For
Toastmasters
Uniquely Delectable
Wake Up A Bland Life
What's Cookin'
Work Of Art
You Can See The Stars In The Kitchen

Your Cup Will Always Be Half Full
Yum's The Word
Yummy
Zesty

Section 3

Art And Magic

"Art museums or art shows in your community can encourage your residents to 'get the picture'. To make it a personal adventure, have them make up stories about each work of art. This will enable you greater insight into their life."

~Pamela Stoltman

Section 3
Art And Magic

"Tutu" Much
…..Blends Seamlessly
A Modern, Chic, Simplicity
Accented
Accentuate
Add Variety
American Original
Ancient Influence
Art 101
Art Of Discovery
Ask The Experts
Be Inspired By A Work Of Art
Blissful
Bold Statement
Calming Waters
Celebrate Contemporary Culture
Check It Out
Cherished Cultural Treasures
Common Denominator
Connecting
Create
Create Your Dream
Cross Culture
Crowd Pleasers
Cultivate
Dark Side
Dawn To Dark
Decadent
Digest
Discover

Dramatic Contrast
Dream
Embellish
Embellishments
Enduring Quality
Enhance
Evoke
Exceeds Expectations
Explore The Differences
Eye On The Past
Feel Like Floating
Feel The Magic
First Impressions
Float
Flourishing
Frou Frou
Get The Picture
Gleam
Heavenly Inspiration
Highlights
Impressive Collection
Initial Reaction
Insight
Inspirational
Inspire Me
Inspired By
Inspired By Art
Inspiring
Jewel Of A Home
Just Take It In
Key Elements
Living Artfully
Look Past The Trees
Luxury Finish

Make It Personal
Makes A Statement
Master
Nature Inspired
Not So Basic
Old World
Old World Designs
One Of The Most Recognizable
Open Spaces
Original Classics
Outdoors Can Be Magical With The Right
Illusions
Paper Airplane And Paper Kites
Peruse
Photo Finish
Picture Perfect
Pizzazz
Poetry In Motion
Pop
Radiating From Within
Redefining
Remarkable
Sense Of Evolution
Set The Scene
Share The Magic
Shear Genius
Sheds Light On Inspiration
Shock Value
Silhouette
Small Wonders
Sparkle And Flair
Structure
Switch It Up
Symmetry

Tangible Embodiment
Tell The Story
Textures
The Art Of The Basic
The Art Of...
The Great Escape
The Resulting Art Is Light Filled
This Land Is Your Land
This Should Be Interesting
Top Picks
Transform
Treasured Gift
Unique Style
Universally
Use Your Skills
Variations On A Theme
Varity
Vast Subjects
Versatile
Viewed To Be The Best
Visual Treat
Whimsical
Why It Works
Wild & Wonderful
Work In Progress
Work Of Art
You'll Never Stop Thinking, Creating &
Imagining

Section 4

Reminiscing And Relationships

"Family means everything to residents. But, be sure to let them know they have several types of families! The one from birth, the one from their life-long or new friends, and the one made of staff! New friendships can be developed with hall partners. Staff can help attain a great relationship with residents by playing a role-reversal or listening to 'romance of the past' and finally, family can strengthen their bond with their loved ones with an event to make things you love, such as a scrapbook of the resident's life."

~Pamela Stoltman

Section 4
Reminiscing And
Relationships

........Of Your Dreams And Desires
A Hand To Guide You
A Mom Should Be Celebrated For A Lifetime
A Twist On Tradition
A Whole New Way To Enjoy
Age Defying
All People Have Something In Common..Now
Discuss
American Treasure
An Inconvenient Truth
Ancient Influences
Antique Alley
Anytime/Anywhere
Anywhere You Are
Acquaint Oneself
Ask The Experts
Basks In The Shadow
Be A Vision Of Romance
Be Beyond The Standard
Be Passionate About Your Roots
Behind The Walls
Beloved
Beloved Love Ones
Best Bets
Blissful Moments
Break Free
By A Thread
Canines With Class

Catch In The Heart
Celebrate Traditions & Stories Of Life
Celebrate Yarn Spinners
Change The Mood
Check It Out
Comfortable And Casual
Compelling Material
Confessions Of A Serial Lover
Connect To Past & Present
Count My Blessings
Create Your Dreams
Curators Of Our Past
Discuss...They Will Have An Opinion
Don't Build A Wall Of Isolation
Don't Just Find Stories...Understand Them
Dreamers Into Doers
Drum Up A Little Nostalgia
Eager To Share
Establish A Bond
Explore The Relationship
Exploring Different Situations
Extra Living
Extra! Extra!
Extraordinary Events Of Life
Extraordinary Life Experiences
Eye Catcher
Eye On The Past
Falling In Love
Falling In Love All Over Again
Family Favorites
Family Friendly
Family Gathering
Famous Friends
Farm Functions

Feel The Magic
Feel The Spirit Of Someone You Love
First Hand Recollections
Flashback
For The Next Generation
Fresh Look W/ Vintage Finds
Gather Around The Table With Those You Love
Gathering Place
Getting Personal
Giggling Is Great
Give Old Things New Uses
Glad You Asked
Golden Age
Gotta Love....
Guest & Glorious.....
Hall Partners
Handle W/ Care
Hands On Adventure
Happy Blurred Kaleidoscope Of Time
Head Over Heels
Hearts On Fire
Hearts Sends Warmest Wishes
Highlights From....
History Lives
Honor The Queen..Even If It Is Queen For A
Day
How Will You Deal With It?
I Learned The Hard Way...Now I Trust My Heart
Imagine The Endless Possibilities
Immerse Yourself In Your Good Times
In The Know
Innovations Through The Years
Inspired Affection
It's Your Turn To Talk

Join Hands And Connect
Keep It Sweet
Keep Yourself Open & Alive
Kit And Caboodle
Lasting Value
Learn Something About People Who Peak In
Narrative
Life 101
Life Happens In A Blink
Listen & Change Everything
Live & Learn
Living History
Lodge Log Living
Long Pauses & Funny Voices
Looking Glass
Loyal
Lullaby
Magic Match
Making It Personal
Matriarchs
Memories
Merry-Go-Round
Mix Old And New
Mommyisms
Neighbor Network
New Ideas
Old Life
Old World
On A Whim
Original Classics
Pennies For....Inflation...A Quarter For Your
Thoughts
People And Place
People Shape & Polish Ordinary Events

Period Settings
Pet Tails/Tales
Pets
Polite Chit Chat
Ready Made Romance
Recollection Of A Special Gift
Respect
Rich History
Rituals
Role Reversal
Romance From The Past
Romantic Details
Round Table Discussion
Round Up
Sassy
See The Big Picture
Send A Little Love
Side By Side
Silhouette
Simple Inspirations
Slow Lane, Slow Love
Slow Methodical Details
Socializing Between Friends
Sought After
Spark The Imagination
Spin A Yarn
Starry-Eyed
Storytelling Festival
Sunny Side Up
Tackle
Tea For Two
Tell Of Bygone Glories
Tell The Story
Telltale Signs

The Balance Of Relationships
The Balance Of Romance
The Beginning Of Something Wonderful
The Best Stories Never End
The Sweetest Life I Know
Things We Love
This Is The Day To Remember
This Should Be Interesting
Thrill Of The Hunt
Through The Glass
Tie The Knot
Translating
Treasure Hunters Discover....
Trip Back In Time
True Companion
Truly Romantic Gesture
Tucked
Ultimate Bonding Experience
Unbridled Passion
Vacation Inspiration
Varieties
Victorian
Vintage
Visions Of Home
We Love It!
Welcome To The Real World
Well Past Childhood And Your Children's
Childhood
When 2 Become 1
Wild Wonders
Winning Hearts
World Class Fun For The Family
Worth Their Salt
Yearn To Be Found Worthy

You Are Better If Understood
You Make It Possible
You've Got To Forgive
Young At Heart
Your Hearts Desire

Section 5

Sensory Programs

"Find ways to delight your residents' senses by including the family with a 'magic of the night' illusion show, or try a cooking class of 'sensational, mouth-filled delicacies that bring the smell of harvests past. You could even host a beautiful musical performance on a patio, 'illuminated with glowing orbs'... Twinkle lights!"

~Pamela Stoltman

Section 5
Sensory Programs

1st Hand Recollections
A Family Affair
Ancient Influences
Anywhere You Are....
Ask The Experts
Atmosphere
Attention Grabbing
Backyard Bouquet
Beauty
Behind The Scenes
Warm & Comfortable
Bubble Head
Call To Mind
Channel Energy
Charmed Life
Choices
Comfortable And Casual
Commit To Memory
Country Classics
Create A Range
Crossed Paths
Discover
Discover Life Radiating From Within
Down To Earth
Dreamy
Elegance
Embrace
Engaging The Mind And The Senses
Envisioning
Explore The Many Sides Of Life

Fall In Rusty Hues
First Impressions
Floating
Generations Upon Generations
Good Deed, Good Fun, Good Read
Gotta Love….
Group Hugs
Hands On Adventure
Home Is Where The Heart Is
If Dreams Could Come True
Illusionary Oasis
In The Know
In The Woods
Indulge Your Sight
Insights
It's A Wrap
Jagged
Just Plain Fun
Key Participants
Life
Life At Home
Life Happens In A Blink
Living Large
Living The Dream
Look For It
Lush And Inviting
Luxurious
Magic
Making It Personal
Memories
Memories Are Made In…..
Morning Breaks Gentle
Music To Your Ears
My Country Life

Oh, Those Clever....
Old World
One For All, All For One
Our Mates
Peace
Pizzazz
Playfulness
Pleasures Of Summer
Politeness
Power Of A Woman
Prickly
Queen For A Day
Read Of The Month
Reason To Smile
Extraordinary Events Of Life
Reflects Your Personality
Romance
Romance Of The Rural Life
Room For Memories
Rush Of Feelings
Sassy
Scouting
Seeing Past The Present
September In The South
Sharp
Sheds New Light On.....Senses
Show Me
Silk Shimmering Over Your Body
So Much More
Soft Touch
Something Wild
Source Of Comfort
Southern Soul
Sparkle

Spin It
Spinning A Yarn
Stirring Up An Sensation
Sweet Heat
Take Two
Tender
Tender Loving Care
Texas Living
Texture
The Best Of Both Worlds
The Blahs
The Sillies
The Briefing
The Face Of Kindness
The Face Of Love
The Face Of Sadness
The Face Of Surprise
The Great Escape
The Heart Of Life
The Touch Of Caring
The Touch Of Gold
The Touch Of Silk
This Land Is Your Land
Top Picks
Trip Back In Time
Tumultuous
Two Worlds Meet To Create An Experience Like
No Other
Unique Culture
Unleash The Force
Velvet Touch
Volume And Shape
Warmth
Welcome To The Real World

Western Bucks And Spurs
What It Takes To Conquer A Day
What's Your Gut Feeling?
Wild Wonders
Winter In The North
Wise Up
Yankee Ingenuity
Ying Yang
You Did It!
Your Skin Is Million Of Sensors That Let You
Feel Your World
Zest

Section 6

Spring And Summer

"Spring is here! Get the residents all stirred up by introducing elements of nature! 'A treasure hunt of botanical beauties are on the grounds of the community!'"

~Pamela Stoltman

Section 6
Spring And Summer

A Walk A Long The Beach
Access To Outside
Afternoons Slowly Easing Into Evenings
Airy
Amazing Blooms
At Last
Basking In The Sun
Block It Out (Sun)
Blossomed
Boiling Point
Botanical Beauties
Branch Out
Bring Inside Out
Butterfly Haven
Catch The Breeze
Celebrate Summer
Change & Renewal
Change Of Season
Clear The Air
Commune With Nature
Cool Junk
Cool Tradition
Cool, Calm, Collected
Dock Tale
Earth Friendly Ideas
Fish Swimming Upstream
Fishing Tackle
Flowers Exist To Make Joy
Fluttering
Fluttering Butterfly

Garden Debut
Garden Fresh
Gear Up For Some Sooth Summer Driving
Gentle Start To Your Morning
Give Me Liberty
Greening Up
Hope Is Blooming
Hot Seat
In The Tree Tops
Introducing Elements Of Nature
Island Attraction
July 4th Flourish
Keep Your Cool
Local Flavor
Make Our Garden Come To Life
Make Summer Come Alive
Morning Silhouette
Natural Match
Old Glory
On The Road Again
Out On A Limb
Out On The Road
Out The Door
Perk Up
Personal Roadmap For Your Life Journey
Pint Size Paradise
Plant It Forward
Pleasures Of America
Quality Time For The Family
Rediscover
Revel In The Grass And Shaded Splendor
Rhythm Of The Woods
Rosy Outlook
Scoops Of Sunshine In Your Hands

Season Of New Beginnings
Shell Seekers
Shoot The Breeze
Show Your Stripes
Showering Us With....
Sink In
Soak Up
Southern Comfort
Southern Sweet
Splendid Surprise
Splish Splash
Springtime
Spur Seaside Memories
Stand Under The Trees
Summer Frazzles
Summer Pleasures
Summer Rite
Summer Splash
Summer Up
Sun Station
Sun Worshippers
Sunsets In An Ever Changing Skyline
Sweat Smart
Sweeping
Sweet Summer
Sweetest Part Of Summer
Take Solace In Deep Moving Water
The Summer's Bet
The Sweet Life
Unwind
Vacation Inspiration
Warming Your Shoulders
Watch The Fire Flies Flicker
Water Yourself

Watermelon Roundup
We'll Color Your World
What's Hot Now
When Heat Overwhelms
You Can Experience The Joy

Section 7

Fall And Winter

"During the colder months, you want your residents to be comfortable and content, so they will not become bored and want to find out what is going on outside, in the cold. Remember the darkness comes earlier in the winter, and the use of 'glowing phrases' on your fliers and daily schedule will help keep the warm and cozy feeling alive. Keep the lights on, and the glitz going for your fast and festive activities."

~Pamela Stoltman

Section 7
Fall And Winter

1st Smells Of Fall
A Cool Autumn Breeze
And Warming Up To…..
As Warm Weather Winds Down
Autumn Assets
Autumn Foliage Tones
Batfest
Beyond Harvest Gold
Can You Hear Fall Calling
Crimson Tide
Dark Side
Double Up
Enchanted Woods
Foreboding
Forgiving Rich Color
Frightening Fun
Gang Of Pumpkins Will Bewitch The Night
Glowing Orbs
Golden Moments
Gusto
Harrowing Handicrafts (Halloween)
Harvest
Harvest Scenes
Hats Off To Texas
In Honor Of The Harvest
Last Golden Rays Of Sun
Magic
Monstrous
Russet
Screeching

Shadows Of The Past
Spirits Of The Night
Taste Of Red Oak
The Flavors Of Fall
The Temp. Is Great, The Leaves Are Beginning
To Glow
Unravel The Mystery
Warm & Cozy
Watchful
Welcome Comforts Of Harvest
Add A Warm Burnished Glow
Adorn
All Aglow
Brightest
Candlelight Cast It's Glow
Celebrate The View
Count Down To Christmas
Cozy Fireplace
Defines The Season
Electrified By Pots Of Gold
Elegantly Adorned
Extra Bit Of Shimmer Makes A Room Sparkle
Fast & Festive
Freeze
Glad Tidings
Glints, Gleams
Glitzy
Glowing
Glows With Warm Welcome
Go For The Glow
Go For The Gold
Going Nuts For Nutcrackers
Holiday Haven
Holiday Merriment

Holiday Sparklers
Holiday Wonderland
Homespun Holidays
Illumination
Joyfulness
Lights Playing
Merry & Bright
Midas Touches
Over-The-Top-Ornamentation
Personally Created To Make Spirits Bright
Right Amount Of Warmth To Cool Places
Seeing Red
Send Holiday Greetings In Style
Sheds New Light On....
Shine On
Simple Pleasures Of The Season
Snow Job
Spaces To Spark.......
Sparkle And Glow
Star Debut
Stars Time
Striking Effect
Stringing Along
Stunning Winter Soiree
Style For The Season
The Best Memories Start Here
The Secret Of Giving
The Wind Is Whipping
Twinkle
Unforgettable Holiday Gala
Whimsical
Winery Tableau
Winter Jewels
Wrapped In Light

Section 8

Outings

"Stretch your legs open your horizons, this land is your land, this land is our land. Come along, and see!"

~Pamela Stoltman

Section 8
Outings

A Few Of Our Favorite Things
A Step At A Time
A Walk In The Woods
All Over The Map
Ancient Influence
Array Of Cultural Events
Bird's Eye View
Book A Complete Escape Today
Call Of The Wild
Calming Waters
Canvas
Captivating
Check It Out
Check Out Our Secret Routes & Favorite Spots
Clean Getaway
Closer Than You Think
Come And Explore A New World
Contact With People You Care About
Counting In The City
Crossed Paths
Discovery Adventure
Don't Miss A Thing
Dream Weavers
Easier Than You Might Have Imagined
Enjoy Each Other's Company
Exotic
Flow
Follow The Lines
For A Much Needed Escape
Fun Factor

Garden Party
Get Going
Get The Ball Rolling
Getting The Goods
Give Me A Field Where The Unmowed Grass Grows
Go The Extra Nautical Mile
Grand Slam Getaways
Happy Feet
Haven
Heading Outdoors
Heart Of The Country
Highly Dramatic
Hit The Road
Impressive Collection
Incredible Destination
Journey Back In Time
Lazy Little River
Legends Tell Of A Rare......
Leisurely Float
Living History
Lush Landscapes
Made In America
Made In The Shade
Meander
Memorable Trip
Navigation Plans
Night On The Town
On The Road Again
One For The Road
Open Your Sense Of Adventure
Out & About
Peaceful Getaway
Perfectly Balanced

Plan Your Trip Now
Practical Tips
Pursue Your Dreams
Put A Smile On Your Face
Relax And Tour
Remarkably
Retro Grade
Right Up Their Alley
Road Trips
Romance Of The Rural Life
Room To Roam
Savvy Spots
Sidewalk Style
Smooth Waters
Something Wild (Zoo)
Special Treatment
Step Into The South
Step Into The World Of Luxury
Stop To Shop
Stretch Your Legs, Open Your Mind
Summer Escape
Sure Bet
Taking The Long View
The Great Escape
The Heart Of Southern Life
There Is Always Something To See Or Do
There's One To Suit Every Fancy
This Is The Day
This Land Is Your Land
Top Picks
Tour The Sights
Travel In Time
Treasured Islands
Underscore

Unique Itineraries
Urban Pleasure
What Women Want
Wild Wonders
Worldly Ways
Worth Exploring

Section 9

Entertainment

"My experience has been that good entertainment goes a log way with residents of all levels. They need to know what is coming, (like, who reads the calendars?) Work to your audience, take a survey, and find out what type of entertainment they like. Sophisticated sparkle, or original classics. Determine this, and they will love you."

~Pamela Stoltman

Section 9
Entertainment

A Class Act
A True Bargain
All Together Now
American Original
Anticipate
Applaud
Appropriate Subject
Are You Ready To Rock?
At Home With History
Attention Gambling
Audience Participation
Beat The Crowds
Best Bets
Big Ideas
Blockbuster
Bold, Bright And Candy Striped
Cameo Appearance
Can't Miss Event
Canopy Of Fun
Center Stage
Concertized
Check It Out
Cherished Cultural Treasures
Chic
Class Act
Contact W/ People You Care About
Country Classics
Crave Excitement
Crowd Pleasers
Cultured Education

Don't Settle For Run Of The Mill
Don't Take A Gamble
Double Feature
Dramatic Contrast
Enamored
Engaging
Enjoy This Very Singular Treat
Ever Involving Image
Exceeds Expectations
Exhilarating
Extra Dose Of Personality
Extra! Extra!
Extraordinary Event
Extravaganza
Famous Friends
First Run Movies
Folks Flock Here Like Birds To A Feather
For Hosting & Toasting
Fresh Lease On Life
Fun House
Games People Play
Get Your Bluegrass On
Getting The Goods
Good Reads
Great For Gathering
Happy Days
Harmony Through Blending
Hat Trick
Hats Off
Highlights From
Highly Dramatic
Ho-Hum
Homespun For The Holidays
Illuminating Conversation

In A Special Light
Introducing
It Will Make A Memory
It's A Wrap
It's Easy To Join... Just Come
Jazz Up
Jazzy
Journey Back In Time
Junk Gypsies
Legendary
Let It Inspire You
Let's Make A Deal
Like A Star
Look For It
Lucky Lunch
Lush And Inviting
Make Time For....
Melodic Journey
Merry Mayhem
Mid Party Boost
Mojo
Must See Event
Never Slumber Party
New Tricks
Nights On The Town
Not Your Typical.......
Off Beat
Oh, Those Clever....
One Last Burst Of Excitement
Only One King Of The Jungle
Options Are Almost Limitless
Original Classics
Pay Homage
People And Place

Planning To Celebrate
Politeness Project
Professional And Personal Favorites
Pull Back The Curtain & Glimpse......
Ready To Deal
Reflects His/Her Personality
Right Up Their Alley
Round Up
Saucy, Sensational & So Much Fun
Save The Date
Seasonal Delights
Share The Best
Share The Magic
Show Me
Showstoppers
Side Step
Simply Festive
Simply The Best
Snap Happy
Snazzy Solution
Soothing Style
Sophisticated Sparkle
Sparkle & Flair
Sparkling Ideas To Celebrate The Season
Special Delivery
Special Treatment
Spot On
Star Spangle Performance
Strut Their Stuff
Stunning
Sugar Coated Holiday
Surprise Package
Swanky
Sweet Inspiration

Sweets & Treats
Take A Bough
Take A Cue
Take A Glimpse
Take Two
Texas Living
The Adventure Begins Today
The Best Of Both Worlds
The Perfect Solution
There's One To Suit Every Fancy
Those Who Are Easily Shocked ...Should Be
Shocked More
Tinkling Fingers
Top It!
Top Picks
Transform
Trendsetters
Trendy
Tried & True
Tune Into Your Environment
Tweaks
Twinkle Toes
Typecast
Ultimate Boredom Buster
Unique
Upcoming
Upscale
Varieties
Vignette
Vivacious Personalities
What's New
Wild Wonders
Winner Circle
Winning Hands

Work Inn Progress
World Class Fun For Everyone
Your Attention, Please
Your Heart's Desire

Section 10

More Words

"It's a great idea to make the most of every day, using tailored words or phrases. This helps to create a bursting, personalized passion in each resident! Don't forget to develop a statement by connecting vast subjects with a common thread."

~Pamela Stoltman

Section 10
More Words

1st Look
A Cut Above
A Few Additions Of Quality Always Bring It Up
A Notch
A Few Of Our Favorite Things
A Plus
A Royal State Of Affairs
A Team W/ A Mission
Accentuate
Accommodate
Accommodating Community
Add Cottage Charm
Add Variety
Added Varity
Aficionado
All In The Details
All That Glitters
All Things Are Possible
All Together Now...
All-Star
Alternative
America's Favorites
American Legacy
Architectural Perfection
Art For All
Ask The Experts
Author's Ink
Avant-Garde
Avowed Motto
Bag It

Bargain Of The Month
Be Patient
Beat The Crowds
Beginning With The Inside Out
Beguiling
Behind The Scenes
Behind The Walls
Benchmark
Best In Show
Best Way To Spend A Day.....
Big Ideas
Blurring The Boards
Bohemian Rhapsody
Bold
Bold Statement
Boot Camp
Brilliant Way To Reveal Joy To Your Life And Landscape
Bring It Home
Bring Sunshine To A Rainy Day
Bring Your Home To Life
Bring Your Living To Life
Browse
Brush Up...
Bucket Of Options
Bull Headed
Bursting
Can't Bear To Be Without
Cash In The Laughs
Classic & Powerful
Catch On
Change Focus
Change Is Good
Chasing Beauty

Check Before You Zero In
Chockablock With Big...
Class Without Compromise
Come And Add Your Energy To Ours
Come To Order
Comfort Zone
Confused
Connect To Something Real
Connect With People You Care About
Cool Junk
Cornering The Market
Count My Blessings
Cover Your Bases
Create A Personalized....
Create A Range
Create Change
Cultivated
Curious
Dare To Explore
Dazed
Deep Thoughts
Delineates
Do Good Days
Do You Believe In Miracles?
Do Your Friends A Favor
Docile
Don't Underestimate.....
Done Deal
Double Up
Down To Earth
Dramatic Contrast
Dramatic Not Traumatic
Draw Inspiration From Imagery & Culture
Durable And Delightful

Easy Indulgence
Effectively
Elegance
Embrace Change
Embrace The Idea
Enough
Escort Service
Essence
Essential Knowledge
Essentials
Establish
Expand Your Horizons
Exquisite Solutions
Extra Measure Of Service
Extra! Extra!
Eye Popping .....Is A Visual Treat
Fable
Fabulously Ornate
Fanciful Sets
Far From Expected
Far-Flung
Farm Followed Function
Faves
Favorite Finds
Favorite Haunts
Final Touches
First Order Of Business
Flip Flop Friday
For A True Experience
For Your Eyes Only
Forefront
Formality
Fresh Thinking
Fringe Benefits

Fruits Of Harvest
Fun & Fab
Fun Factor
Get Involved
Get The Skinny
Get With The Plan
Getting There
Getting To Your Good Place
Giddy Up
Gift Of Good Taste
Go Beyond The Ordinary
Goddess
Going Crackers
Good & Easy
Good Deal
Good Standard
Great Moments In History
Great Pick
Great Quotes From Great Minds
Green W/ Envy
Handful Of......
Hang Tight
Has Wooded Generations
Hat Happy
Hat Trick
Healing Ritual
Heavenly
Heavenly Inspiration
Hefty
Helping Hands
Hidden Joys
Hidden Talent
Hip & Historic
Hip To Be Square

Hissy Fit
Hold Everything
Hold The Line
Home Is Where The Heart Is
Homegrown Education
Hot Stuff
Hot Topics
Hot Trends
Hungry For Something Special
If You Dare
Improvise
In A Flash
Indispensable
Indulge Your Passion For...
Infinite Possibilities
Ingenious Solutions
Inner Circle
Innovations
Inside Access
Inspire Me
Interlude
It's A Cinch
It's A Miracle
It's Your Move
Journey Back
Jump In
Jumping Through Hoops
Keep Discovering
Keep It Real
Kindred Spirits
Lady Luck
Let's Make A Deal
Letter Perfect
Letting Go

Level Best
Life 101
Life At Home
Life On The Wild Side
Light The Way
Light Up The Room
Little Sophisticate
Live The Sparkling Life
Look What I Found
Looking For Some Action
Lovely Gesture
Made In The Shade
Make A Statement
Make A Statement Without Saying A Word
Make It Your Own
Making The Most Of Everyday
Market Place
Marveling
Massive
Men Will Be Boys
Mix & Match
Mix Old And New
Modern Twist
Money Matters
Monkey See, Monkey Do
More Choices For Life Well Spent
Morning Glory
Most Wanted
Narrow Margins
Natural Sense
Nature & History Dictate
Near Peak
Neutral
News Flash

Newsflash
Nose Around
Notable In Suggesting
Nothing-To-It
Now You're Talking
Now You're Thinking
Number Crunch
Obelisks
Off To The Races
Often And With Verve
Oh, So Simple
Old & Improved
Old School Elegance
Old World Designs
On The Cutting Edge
One Good Deed
One-On-One Time
Open Door Policy
Opportunity To Meditate
Options Are Almost Limitless
Organized And Effortless
Organized Effort
Paper Perfect
Patroness
Peek-A-Boo
Perfect First Steps
Personality Parade
Peruse
Pet Stop
Phantom
Pick One...Just One
Piece Of History
Pin Up Girl
Pit Stop

Playful Parcels
Portrait Of America
Practical Tips
Preened
Present Perfect
Presto
Pretty, Yet Practical
Prime Time
Put A Smile On
Quest Fulfilled
Quick & Easy
Quirk
Rainbow Connection
Rampant
Reach For The Sky
Ready, Set, Relax
Respect
Rest Upon Their Laurels
Reuse
Rich Neutral Backdrop
Rodeo Roundup
Roped In
Round Up Of Smart Talk
Royal Luxury
Running Headlong Into....
Safety Is Number 1
Saturated
Saturation Point
Savor The Journey
Scoop
Seeing Past The Present
Seen & Heard
Serene Comfort
Serene Scene

Shades Of Autumn
Shaping Our World And History
Share The Bet
Share Top Finds
She's Gotta Have It
Shear Genius
Shopping Connection
Sign Of The Zodiac
Simply Exquisite
Skirt The Issue
Slam Dunk
Small Changes..Big Impact
Smile, You're Amazing
Snack Attack
Snap Happy
Soaring Score
Special Delivery
Special Touché That Make Your Day Complete
Special Treatment
Spread The Word
Standards Set The Highest In The Industry
Step Into The World Of Luxury
Step Up A Notch
Stick To It
Sticky Situation
Store In Style
Straight Laced
Straight, True, Trusted
Strength In Numbers
Stress Management
Striking Costumes
Strong Silent Type
Sturdy
Stymied

Sum It Up
Summon Up
Sure Shots
Surf & Learn
Surround Yourself With An Array Of Love And
Laughter
Sweet Dreams
Swingin' Good Times
Switch Hit
Swooped
Table Talk
Tackle
Take In The View
Take Note
Take Two
Taking The Time
Talking The Talk
Taming The Beast
Taste Of Success
Teamwork
The Art Of Inspiration
The Beginning Of Something Wonderful
The Briefing
The Finer Things In Life
The Heart Of Southern Life
The Moves Are For You
The Perfect Blend
The Perfect Solution
The Quality You Expect..The Life You Enjoy
The Real Deal
The Right Time
The Soul Of The South Is It's People..You'll Fit
Right In
The Sweet Life

Then & Now
Think Before You Write
Think Fast
Think Pink
Think Small
This Is The Day
Tidy Transition
Time After Time
Time Out
To The Rescue
To Thine Own Self Be True
Today's Lifestyle
Toe The Line
Top It
Top Picks
Tour The Sights
Transform
Treasure Chest
Trendsetters
Tres Chic
True Blue
Unabashedly Opulent
Understanding The Risks
Unique Perspective
Unprecedented Exhibition
Unpredictable
Up Close View Of History
Urban Pleasure
Utilitarian
Value Is The Luxury
Variations On A Theme
Vast Subjects
Versatile
Vintage

Voice Of Hope
Walk This Way
Warm & Comforting
We Love To Share Food, Stories And
Advice..Whether You Ask For It Or Not
We'll Make You Feel Right At Home
Welcome Addition
Well Contained
What A Deal
What A Great Idea!
What You Need To Know
What's New
What's New ...What's Next?
What's Next?
What's On Your Horizon
What's Right For You...Right Now
When Life Give You A Lemon
Where Only Eagles Dare
Where Woman Create
Whittle
Who Will Make The First Move
Wild, Wild West
Wing It
Winning Hand
Wise Up
Words From The Wise
Words To Live By
Work In Progress
Worth Cheering For
Wow Them With Details
Write On
You Were Born Ready
Young At Heart

Your Circle Of Friends Just Got A Whole Lot
Bigger
Your Cup Will Always Be Half Full

Section 11

Catchy Sayings

"Bring sunshine to a rainy day by asking the residents to complete sentences. Another idea is to ask residents what these catchy sayings mean to them. Your residents' minds benefit from this kind of thinking and creation!"

~Pamela Stoltman

Section 11
Catchy Sayings

A Great Idea Is Worth Sharing

A Warm Smile & A Spoonful Of Care Are The Best Prescription For Keeping You Well.

Always Arrive In Style

An Unexpected Turn Can Lead To A Hidden Discovery

Be One In A Million Not One Of A Million.

Brighten Every Day W/ Fun Finds That Make You Smile.

Clear Vision Helps To Eliminate The Indecisiveness That Can Result In Countless Irritating Difficulties.

Close Friendship Can Effect How Well And Even How Long We Live!

Create A Treat That Is As Aromatic As Is Visual

DO You See Emptiness Or Possibilities

Draw Guests Among The Paths To The Pavilion Where They Are Welcomed With Drink & Hors D' Oeuvres

Dreamers Into Doers

Everyone Deserves A Little Luxury

Few Things Are Prettier Than The Warm Glow Of Tiny Lights Filtered Through The Evergreen Branched Of A Blanket Of Snow.

Find That Unique Holiday Gift That Is Not Easily Forgotten

For An Abundant Forest Tomorrow, Plant It Forward Today.

Give An Old Idea New Purpose

Golden Toasted And Perfectly Cheesy (Entertainment)

Happiness Is Always In Season

Make An Ideal Setting To Watch The Sun Dance Lazily Down

If You Pack Your Patience You Will End Up With Memories That Can Never Be Replaced!

If...?

Image Of Youthful Innocence & Anticipation Are The Essence Of The Season.

It Only Looks Like The Real Thing

It Will Bring Sunshine To A Rainy Day

It'll Remind You Again And Again Why Your
Memory Is A Gem Like No Other.

It's What Separates You From……..

Just Go For It …It Will Make You So Happy

Keep Your Eyes On The Prize

Let Us Never Forget That The Cultivation Of
The Earth Is The Most Important Labor Of Man.
The Farmer, Therefore, Is The Founder Of
Civilization.

Let Us Remind You Of A Simple Truth: Grand
Adventures Can Begin Right Here At Home.

Life Is But A Dream

Life Is Full Of Celebrations

Listen Carefully To That Little Voice In You

Live The Life W/O Paying The Price

Love And Memories Of Holidays Past Are The
Threads That Tie Us To Holidays Present..

Make A Relaxed Pace That Invites And Ignites
Exploration

Make Memories They All Will Treasure Forever

My Garden Of Flowers Is Also My Garden Of Thoughts And Dreams.

Nature Does Not Hurry, Yet Everything Is Accomplished

Nothing Like A Young Child To Bring Back The Excitement To The Season.

Now Your Wildest Dreams Can Take Flight.

Only Light Seen For Miles Beneath The Blackberry-Colored Sky.

Our Dress Code: Wear Something.

Perfection Cannot Be Attained, But That's No Reason To Stop Trying.

Pure Opulence For The Memorable Moments In Your Life

Real Security Is Knowing You're At Home At The Lodge.

Savor The Height Of Summer W/ Fun & Festivities.

Scholars Ranked It As...

Send Out Wishes For Peace On This Troubled Earth

Served With Great Panache, Tempered By Classic Good Taste

Shopping Opportunities You Won't Want To Miss.

Some Of The Best Moments Are Small Ones

Strategies That Have Proven Themselves Over The Long Term.

Summer Pleasures Are Highlighted By Anticipation Of Fall

Take Advantage Of The Exceptional Service.

The Best Way To Roast A Chicken Is To Let Someone Else Does It!

The Best Way To Roast A Chicken Is To Let Someone Else Does It!

The Feelings Of Attraction Have Never Been So Strong.

The Only Person You Can Change Is Yourself

The Tradition Dates To The Early Days Of Our Ancestors

There Is No Such Thing As Being Too Safe

They Always Say "Time Changes Things", But You Actually Have To Change Them Yourself

Time Constraints Of Our Modern Lifestyles

Trust The Champion For Certified Success.

Turn On Your Music, And Time Has A Purpose.

Understand The Risks See The Benefits.

Want To Be In The Center Of Action: See & Be Seen

When It Comes To Aging We Think Outside The Box

Who Needs To Be Young When So Many Of Your Friends Are?

Quick Reference

Quick Reference
Wellness/Health /Beauty Programs

Quick Reference
Food

Quick Reference

Art And Magic

Quick Reference
Reminiscing And Relationships

106

Quick Reference
Sensory Programs

Quick Reference

Spring And Summer

Quick Reference
Fall

Quick Reference
Winter

Quick Reference

Outings

Quick Reference

Entertainment

Quick Reference
More Words

Quick Reference
Catchy Sayings

Quick Reference
Other

At-A-Glance
Matrix

	Art & Magic	Fall & Winter	Entertainment	Food	Outings	Reminiscence & Relationships	Sensory	Spring & Summer	Wellness/Health/Beauty	Marketing
...Blends Seamlessly	●			●		●	●			
...Of Your Dreams And Desires	●	●	●	●	●	●				
"Tutu" Much	●		●							
1st Hand Recollections	●	●		●		●	●	●	●	
1st Look	●		●		●		●		●	
1st Smells Of Fall		●				●	●	●		
A Brand New View	●		●		●	●			●	
A Class Act			●	●	●	●			●	
A Cool Autumn Breeze		●				●	●	●		
A Cut Above	●		●	●	●				●	
A Dramatic Mix	●	●	●	●	●	●	●	●	●	
A Family Affair	●	●	●	●	●	●	●	●	●	
A Few Additions Of Quality Always Bring It Up A Notch										●
A Few Of Our Favorite Things					●					
A Hand To Guide You	●		●	●	●		●		●	
A Modern, Chic, Simplicity	●									
A Mom Should Be Celebrated For A Lifetime	●					●		●	●	
A Plus		●	●	●		●		●	●	
A Royal State Of Affairs	●		●	●	●					
A Step At A Time	●		●			●	●	●	●	
A Taste For The Extraordinary				●						
A Team W/ A Mission		●	●	●	●	●			●	
A True Bargain	●		●	●	●	●				
A Twist On Tradition	●	●	●	●			●		●	
A Vision Of Timeless Beauty									●	

	Art & Magic	Fall & Winter	Entertainment	Food	Outings	Reminiscence & Relationships	Sensory	Spring & Summer	Wellness/Health/Beauty	Marketing
...Blends Seamlessly	●			●		●	●			
...Of Your Dreams And Desires	●	●	●	●	●	●				
"Tutu" Much	●		●							
1st Hand Recollections	●	●		●		●	●	●	●	
1st Look	●		●		●		●		●	
1st Smells Of Fall		●				●	●	●		
A Brand New View	●		●			●	●		●	
A Class Act			●	●		●	●		●	
A Cool Autumn Breeze		●				●	●	●		
A Cut Above	●		●	●	●				●	
A Dramatic Mix	●	●	●	●	●	●	●	●	●	
A Family Affair	●	●	●	●	●	●	●	●	●	
A Few Additions Of Quality Always Bring It Up A Notch										●
A Few Of Our Favorite Things				●						
A Hand To Guide You	●		●	●	●		●		●	
A Modern, Chic, Simplicity	●									
A Mom Should Be Celebrated For A Lifetime	●					●		●	●	
A Plus		●	●	●		●		●	●	
A Royal State Of Affairs	●		●	●	●					
A Step At A Time	●		●			●	●	●	●	
A Taste For The Extraordinary				●						
A Team W/ A Mission		●	●	●	●	●			●	
A True Bargain	●		●	●	●	●				
A Twist On Tradition	●	●	●	●			●		●	
A Vision Of Timeless Beauty									●	

	Art & Magic	Fall & Winter	Entertainment	Food	Outings	Reminiscence & Relationships	Sensory	Spring & Summer	Wellness/Health/Beauty	Marketing
A Walk A Long The Beach					●	●	●	●	●	
A Walk In The Woods		●			●	●	●	●	●	
A Whole New Way To Enjoy	●		●	●	●		●		●	
A Winning Combination				●						
Abundant Experience		●		●						
Accented	●									
Accentuate	●	●	●	●		●	●	●	●	
Access To Outside		●	●	●	●	●	●	●	●	
Accommodate	●		●		●	●			●	
Accommodating Community										●
Achieve									●	
Acquaint Oneself						●				
Acts Of Kindness						●	●			
Add A Warm Burnished Glow		●		●	●	●	●	●	●	
Add Cottage Charm		●		●	●		●	●		
Add Variety	●	●							●	
Adorn	●	●		●		●	●		●	
Adventure						●	●			
Aficionado			●		●	●	●		●	
Afternoons Slowly Easing Into Evenings								●		
Age Defying			●		●	●	●		●	
Aged To Perfection	●			●		●	●		●	
Airy	●	●			●	●	●	●		
All Aglow	●	●				●	●	●	●	
All In The Details						●	●			

	Art & Magic	Fall & Winter	Entertainment	Food	Outings	Reminiscence & Relationships	Sensory	Spring & Summer	Wellness/Health/Beauty	Marketing
All Over The Map					●					
All People Have Something In Common..Now Discuss						●				
All That Glitters	●	●	●				●		●	
All The Trimmings		●		●						
All Things Are Possible	●		●			●			●	
All Together Now	●		●		●	●	●		●	
All-Star		●	●	●	●				●	
Alternative	●		●	●	●	●	●		●	
Amazing Blooms								●		
Amazing Grace		●								
America's Favorites			●	●		●				
American Legacy			●			●				
American Original	●		●	●		●	●	●	●	
American Treasure	●	●	●	●	●	●	●	●	●	
Amplify Natural Beauty			●				●		●	
An Inconvenient Truth	●		●	●		●				
An Ode To Abundance		●								
Ancient Influences	●	●		●	●	●	●	●	●	
And Warming Up To.....		●	●	●			●	●	●	
Anticipate	●	●	●	●	●	●	●	●	●	
Antique Alley	●		●		●	●	●			
Anytime/Anywhere	●		●	●		●	●		●	
Anywhere You Are....	●		●	●	●	●	●		●	
Applaud			●							
Appropriate Subject			●							

	Art & Magic	Fall & Winter	Entertainment	Food	Outings	Reminiscence & Relationships	Sensory	Spring & Summer	Wellness/Health/Beauty	Marketing
Architectural Perfection	●				●	●				
Are You Ready To Rock?			●	●	●					
Area Of Environment	●	●	●	●	●	●	●	●		
Array Of Chic									●	
Array Of Cultural Events	●		●		●	●	●			
Art 101	●									
Art For All	●		●		●	●	●			
Art Of Discovery	●		●	●	●	●	●		●	
As Warm Weather Winds Down		●		●	●	●	●			
Ask The Experts	●		●	●	●	●	●		●	●
At 1st Blush				●						
At Home With History			●							
At Last								●		
Atmosphere		●	●	●	●	●	●	●	●	
Attention Grabbing	●		●	●		●	●		●	
Audience Participation	●		●	●	●	●	●		●	
Authentic Inspiration						●	●			
Author's Ink										
Autumn Assets		●	●	●	●	●	●		●	
Autumn Foliage Tones		●			●	●	●		●	
Autumn Spin On....		●								
Avant-Garde	●								●	
Avowed Motto						●			●	
Baby Boo's		●								
Backyard Bouquet	●	●		●	●	●	●	●		

	Art & Magic	Fall & Winter	Entertainment	Food	Outings	Reminiscence & Relationships	Sensory	Spring & Summer	Wellness/Health/Beauty	Marketing
Bag It				●			●			
Baking Memories				●						
Bargain Of The Month										
Basks In The Shadow			●		●		●	●		
Batfest		●	●		●	●				
Be A Happiness Projector									●	
Be A Vision Of Romance						●				
Be Beyond The Standard						●				
Be Inspired By A Work Of Art	●		●	●		●	●		●	
Be Passionate About Your Roots						●				
Be Patient			●			●	●		●	
Be Well									●	
Bear In Mind						●	●			
Beat The Crowds			●							●
Beat The Heat With Some Frozen Treats And Icy Cold Drinks				●	●		●	●		
Beauty	●	●		●		●	●	●	●	
Beauty And Timeless Style	●				●	●	●		●	
Beauty Tune-up									●	
Beginning With The Inside Out	●				●			●		
Beguiling			●			●				
Behind The Scenes	●		●	●		●	●		●	
Behind The Walls	●					●			●	
Beloved						●				
Beloved Love Ones						●				
Benchmark			●	●		●			●	

	Art & Magic	Fall & Winter	Entertainment	Food	Outings	Reminiscence & Relationships	Sensory	Spring & Summer	Wellness/Health/Beauty	Marketing
Best Bets	●	●	●	●	●	●	●	●	●	
Best In Show			●		●	●			●	
Best Way To Spend A Day.....			●		●				●	
Beware!		●								
Bewitching		●								
Bewitching "Boo" Fest		●								
Beyond Harvest Gold		●			●	●	●			
Big Event			●							
Big Ideas	●	●	●	●	●	●	●	●	●	
Big Top			●							
Biggest Mistakewarm & Comfortable						●	●			
Bird Feasting		●								
Bird's Eye View	●				●	●	●			
Bite You Back		●								
Black Beauties		●								
Black Bounty		●								
Black Magic		●								
Blissful	●									
Blissful Moments						●				
Block It Out (Sun)					●			●	●	
Blockbuster	●		●	●	●	●			●	
Blossomed		●			●	●	●	●		
Blurring The Boards			●			●				
Bohemian Rhapsody			●			●	●			
Boil & Bubble Some Trouble		●								

	Art & Magic	Fall & Winter	Entertainment	Food	Outings	Reminiscence & Relationships	Sensory	Spring & Summer	Wellness/Health/Beauty	Marketing
Boiling Point				●			●			
Bold	●	●	●	●			●		●	
Bold Statement	●	●		●	●	●		●	●	
Bold, Bright And Candy Striped			●							
Bold, Whimsical & Flirty									●	
Book A Complete Escape Today	●		●		●		●		●	
Boot Camp		●			●	●		●	●	
Botanical Beauties		●			●	●	●	●		
Bottom Line						●	●			
Branch Out								●		
Break Free						●				
Break From Tradition		●								
Break Out									●	
Breeze Out For Lunch				●	●					
Brew Ha Ha Punch		●								
Brightest	●	●	●		●		●	●		
Brilliant Balance									●	
Brilliant Way To Reveal Joy To Your Life And Landscape										●
Bring Fireworks To The Table			●	●	●			●		
Bring Inside Out								●		
Bring It Home										●
Bring Sunshine To A Rainy Day										●
Bring Your Home To Life										●
Bring Your Living To Life										●
Browse	●				●				●	

	Art & Magic	Fall & Winter	Entertainment	Food	Outings	Reminiscence & Relationships	Sensory	Spring & Summer	Wellness/Health/Beauty	Marketing
Brush Up...	●		●			●			●	
Bubble Head	●		●			●	●		●	
Bucket Of Options				●	●				●	
Building Independent Skills									●	
Bull Headed			●		●	●				
Burger Boutique				●						
Bursting	●	●	●	●		●	●	●	●	
Butterfly Haven					●		●	●		
By A Thread						●	●		●	
By The Sea		●								
By The Season		●								
Call Of The Wild					●					
Call To Mind	●	●	●	●	●	●	●	●	●	
Calming Sensation	●	●	●	●	●	●	●	●	●	
Calming Waters	●				●				●	
Cameo Appearance			●							
Can You Hear Fall Calling		●			●		●	●		
Can't Bear To Be Without										
Can't Miss Event			●							
Candlelight Cast It's Glow		●				●	●		●	
Canines With Class						●				
Canopy Of Fun			●	●	●			●		
Canvas	●		●	●	●				●	
Captivating	●	●	●	●	●	●	●	●	●	
Care Of Yourself				●					●	

	Art & Magic	Fall & Winter	Entertainment	Food	Outings	Reminiscence & Relationships	Sensory	Spring & Summer	Wellness/Health/Beauty	Marketing
Carefree Countdown									●	
Carry On						●	●			
Carved Ice		●								
Cash In The Laughs										
Catch In The Heart	●		●			●	●			
Catch On										
Catch The Breeze		●			●	●	●	●		
Celebrate Contemporary Culture	●		●	●	●					
Celebrate Summer								●		
Celebrate The Harvest		●								
Celebrate The View	●	●			●		●	●		
Celebrate Traditions & Stories Of Life						●				
Celebrate Yarn Spinners						●				
Center Stage	●		●	●	●	●				
Challenge									●	
Challenge Yourself									●	
Change & Renewal		●	●	●		●		●	●	
Change Focus			●	●	●	●	●		●	●
Change Is Good				●	●				●	●
Change Of Season		●		●	●	●	●	●	●	
Change The Mood						●				
Channel Energy					●	●	●		●	
Character Builder									●	
Charmed Life						●	●		●	
Chasing Beauty			●			●			●	

	Art & Magic	Fall & Winter	Entertainment	Food	Outings	Reminiscence & Relationships	Sensory	Spring & Summer	Wellness/Health/Beauty	Marketing
Check Before You Zero In				●			●			
Check It Out	●		●	●	●	●	●		●	
Check Out Our Secret Routes & Favorite Spots				●	●				●	
Cheer Factor				●	●	●	●	●	●	
Cherished Cultural Treasures	●			●	●	●			●	
Chic				●					●	
Chockablock With Big...	●		●	●					●	
Chocolate Lovers Rejoice				●						
Choices	●		●	●	●	●	●		●	
Class Act			●							
Class Without Compromise			●			●			●	●
Classic & Powerful			●			●	●		●	●
Classic Beauty									●	
Clean Getaway					●	●				
Clear The Air								●		
Clear Vision									●	
Closer Than You Think		●	●		●			●		
Collective Wisdom						●	●			
Colorful Flavors				●						
Come And Add Your Energy To Ours										●
Come And Explore A New World	●	●	●	●	●		●	●	●	
Come Hungry				●						
Come To Order	●								●	
Comfort Zone				●		●	●		●	
Comfortable And Casual				●	●	●	●			

	Art & Magic	Fall & Winter	Entertainment	Food	Outings	Reminiscence & Relationships	Sensory	Spring & Summer	Wellness/Health/Beauty	Marketing
Commit To Memory	●					●	●		●	
Common Denominator	●	●	●	●	●	●	●	●	●	
Commune With Nature								●		
Compelling Material						●				
Concertized			●			●	●		●	
Confessions Of A Serial Lover	●					●			●	
Confused			●			●	●			
Connect To Past & Present						●				
Connect To Something Real	●		●		●				●	●
Connect With People You Care About										●
Connecting	●									
Contact W/ People You Care About			●		●					
Cookie Forest		●		●						
Cool Junk								●		
Cool Pumpkin Patch		●								
Cool Tradition								●		
Cool, Calm, Collected								●		
Cornering The Market	●		●	●		●			●	
Count Down To Christmas	●	●	●	●	●	●	●			
Count My Blessings						●	●		●	
Counter Intelligence						●	●			
Counting In The City					●					
Country Christmas		●								
Country Classics			●	●	●	●	●	●		
Cover Your Bases			●		●	●			●	●

	Art & Magic	Fall & Winter	Entertainment	Food	Outings	Reminiscence & Relationships	Sensory	Spring & Summer	Wellness/Health/Beauty	Marketing
Cozy Fireplace		●				●	●			
Crave Excitement			●							
Create	●									
Create A Personalized....	●			●						
Create A Range	●			●		●	●		●	
Create Your Dream Holiday		●								
Create Your Dreams	●					●				
Crimson Tide		●		●	●	●	●	●		
Crisp Fall Evening		●								
Cross Culture	●		●	●	●	●	●		●	
Crossed Paths			●		●	●			●	
Crowd Pleasers	●		●							
Culinary Classics				●						
Cultivate	●		●	●		●	●		●	
Cultured Education			●							
Curators Of Our Past	●					●	●			
Curious	●	●	●	●	●	●	●	●	●	●
Dance Through Greece				●						
Dare To Explore	●	●	●	●	●	●	●	●	●	
Dark Side	●	●				●			●	
Dawn To Dark	●									
Dazed			●		●	●	●		●	
Deals & Steals		●				●	●			
Dear Taste Buds We've Been Thinking About You				●						
Decadent	●		●	●	●	●			●	

	Art & Magic	Fall & Winter	Entertainment	Food	Outings	Reminiscence & Relationships	Sensory	Spring & Summer	Wellness/Health/Beauty	Marketing
Deep Thoughts	●					●	●		●	●
Defines The Season		●	●	●	●	●	●	●		
Delectable			●	●	●	●	●		●	
Desk Your Halls		●								
Devilish Décor		●								
Digest	●									
Dinner For Two				●						
Disarm W/ Charm									●	
Discover	●	●	●	●	●	●	●	●	●	
Discover Life Radiating From Within		●		●		●	●	●	●	
Discovery Adventure					●					
Discuss…They Will Have An Opinion						●				
Ditch The Negative Emotions									●	
Do Good Days		●	●	●	●	●	●	●		●
Do You Believe In Miracles?	●					●			●	●
Do Your Friends A Favor										●
Docile						●	●		●	
Dock Tale					●	●	●	●		
Don't Build A Wall Of Isolation						●				
Don't Have To Look Old Hat		●			●	●	●	●	●	
Don't Ignore It			●							
Don't Just Find Stories…Understand Them						●				
Don't Miss A Thing					●					
Don't Settle For Run Of The Mill			●	●	●	●			●	
Don't Stereotype Me									●	

	Art & Magic	Fall & Winter	Entertainment	Food	Outings	Reminiscence & Relationships	Sensory	Spring & Summer	Wellness/Health/Beauty	Marketing
Don't Take A Gamble			●							
Don't Underestimate.....	●	●	●	●	●	●	●	●	●	●
Done Deal	●		●	●	●	●	●		●	●
Double Feature			●							
Double Up					●	●			●	
Down Home				●						
Down To Earth			●	●	●	●	●	●	●	
Downright Devilish		●								
Dramatic Contrast	●		●							
Dramatic Not Traumatic	●		●	●	●	●				
Draw Inspiration From Imagery & Culture	●		●	●	●	●				
Dream	●		●	●		●	●			
Dream Weavers			●			●	●		●	
Dreamers Into Doers						●			●	
Dreamy	●	●	●	●	●	●	●	●		
Dressed To Kill			●		●	●				
Drum Up A Little Nostalgia	●	●	●	●	●	●	●	●	●	
Durable And Delightful	●		●						●	
Eager To Share	●		●	●	●	●			●	
Earth Friendly Ideas		●		●	●	●	●	●	●	
Earth Tones		●								
Easier Than You Might Have Imagined					●	●			●	
Easy Indulgence		●	●	●	●	●	●			●
Easy, Local And Flavorful	●		●	●	●	●	●			
Eat Well To Night				●						

	Art & Magic	Fall & Winter	Entertainment	Food	Outings	Reminiscence & Relationships	Sensory	Spring & Summer	Wellness/Health/Beauty	Marketing
Eat, Drink & Be Scary		●								
Eat, Pray, Love				●		●	●		●	
Edible Blooms				●						
Eerie Darkness		●								
Effectively	●		●		●				●	
Electrified By Pots Of Gold	●	●		●			●	●		
Elegance	●		●	●	●	●	●		●	
Elegantly Adorned		●		●				●		
Embellishments	●	●	●	●						
Embrace	●		●	●	●	●	●		●	
Embrace Change										●
Embrace The Idea						●			●	
Enamored		●	●			●	●			
Enchanted Woods		●			●	●		●		
Endlessly Glamorous									●	
Enduring Beauty	●	●	●			●	●		●	
Energetic Chaos	●		●		●	●				
Engaging			●			●	●			
Engaging The Mind And The Senses	●	●	●	●	●	●	●	●	●	
Enhance	●									
Enjoy Each Other's Company					●					
Enjoy This Very Singular Treat			●	●	●	●	●			
Enough				●		●			●	
Entice	●		●	●					●	
Envisioning	●					●	●		●	

	Art & Magic	Fall & Winter	Entertainment	Food	Outings	Reminiscence & Relationships	Sensory	Spring & Summer	Wellness/Health/Beauty	Marketing
Epicurean Knowledge			●	●	●		●			
Escort Service					●					
Essence	●	●	●	●	●	●	●	●	●	
Essential Knowledge	●		●	●	●	●			●	●
Essentials	●		●	●	●	●	●		●	
Establish				●					●	
Establish A Bond						●				
Ever Involving Image			●							
Every Taste Has A Feeling				●						
Everyday Confidence									●	
Everyone Is Jumping									●	
Evoke	●									
Exceeds Expectations	●		●	●	●	●	●		●	
Exhilarating	●	●	●	●	●	●	●	●	●	
Exotic	●		●	●	●					
Expand Your Horizons	●	●	●	●	●	●	●	●	●	●
Experience The Classic Beauty									●	
Experience The Flavor				●						
Explore The Differences	●									
Explore The Many Sides Of Life	●	●	●	●	●	●	●	●	●	
Explore The Relationship						●			●	
Explore The Taste				●						
Exploring Different Situations						●				
Express Your Style									●	
Exquisite Solutions			●	●	●	●	●		●	●

	Art & Magic	Fall & Winter	Entertainment	Food	Outings	Reminiscence & Relationships	Sensory	Spring & Summer	Wellness/Health/Beauty	Marketing
Extra Bit Of Shimmer Makes A Room Sparkle		●				●	●	●		
Extra Living						●				
Extra Measure Of Service										●
Extra! Extra!			●	●	●				●	
Extraordinary Events		●	●							
Extraordinary Events Of Life			●	●	●	●	●			
Extraordinary Life Experiences						●				
Extravagant		●								
Extravaganza			●							
Eye Catcher	●		●	●						
Eye On The Past	●	●	●	●	●	●	●	●	●	
Eye Popping .....Is A Visual Treat	●		●		●					
Fable	●	●	●			●	●	●		
Fabulously Ornate	●	●	●	●	●	●		●		
Fairy Tale			●							
Fall Foliage In Full Bloom		●								
Fall In Rusty Hues		●			●	●	●			
Falling In Love						●	●		●	
Falling In Love All Over Again						●	●		●	
Family Favorites			●	●	●	●				
Family Friendly			●	●	●				●	
Family Gathering		●	●	●	●	●		●		
Famous Friends			●			●				
Fanciful Foods				●		●	●		●	
Fanciful Sets			●		●	●	●			

	Art & Magic	Fall & Winter	Entertainment	Food	Outings	Reminiscence & Relationships	Sensory	Spring & Summer	Wellness/Health/Beauty	Marketing
Far From Expected	●		●	●	●	●	●		●	●
Far-Flung			●		●	●				
Farm Functions		●		●	●	●		●		
Fast & Festive			●	●	●	●				
Faves	●	●	●	●	●	●	●	●	●	
Favorite Finds	●				●	●	●		●	●
Favorite Haunts	●				●	●				
Feel Like A Star			●			●	●		●	
Feel Like Floating	●									
Feel The Difference									●	
Feel The Magic	●	●				●				
Feel The Spirit Of Someone You Love						●				
Feeling Great!									●	
Feeling Sluggish									●	
Fiendish Fun		●								
Final Touches	●		●	●	●	●	●		●	
Fired Up For Dinner				●	●	●	●			
Fireside Supper		●								
First Hand Recollections	●	●	●	●	●	●	●	●	●	
First Impressions	●		●			●	●			
First Order Of Business						●			●	
First Run Movies			●		●	●				
Fish Swimming Upstream					●	●	●	●		
Fishing Tackle					●	●	●			
Flashback	●	●	●	●	●	●	●	●	●	

	Art & Magic	Fall & Winter	Entertainment	Food	Outings	Reminiscence & Relationships	Sensory	Spring & Summer	Wellness/Health/Beauty	Marketing
Flavor Your World			●	●	●					
Flawless									●	
Flip Flop Friday			●		●			●		
Float				●	●		●	●		
Floating	●			●	●	●	●			
Flock From All Over The Country Side			●							
Flourishing		●		●	●	●	●	●	●	
Flow	●		●		●	●	●	●	●	
Flowers Exist To Make Joy		●			●	●	●	●	●	
Fluttering	●	●					●	●		
Fluttering Butterfly								●		
Focus	●					●	●		●	
Folks Flock Here Like Birds To A Feather			●	●					●	
Follow The Lines	●				●	●	●		●	
Food Finds		●		●	●	●	●	●	●	
Food For Thought				●						
For A Much Needed Escape			●		●				●	
For A True Experience	●		●	●	●	●	●		●	●
For Hosting & Toasting			●							
For The Love Of ...Apples				●						
For The Next Generation	●		●	●		●			●	
For Your Eyes Only	●		●			●	●			
Foreboding						●				
Forefront	●					●	●		●	
Forgiving Rich Color	●	●		●	●	●	●	●		

	Art & Magic	Fall & Winter	Entertainment	Food	Outings	Reminiscence & Relationships	Sensory	Spring & Summer	Wellness/Health/Beauty	Marketing
Formality										
Frame Of Mind	●		●	●	●	●	●			
Freeze		●		●		●	●			
Freeze Frame				●						
French Connection				●						
French Frills			●	●	●	●	●			
Fresh				●						
Fresh Lease On Life			●							
Fresh Look W/ Vintage Finds	●		●		●	●			●	
Fresh New You									●	
Fresh Picks				●						
Fresh Start	●			●					●	
Fresh Thinking	●		●	●	●		●	●	●	
Fresh Vitality									●	
Freshen Up Your.....									●	
Fresher Thinking			●	●		●			●	●
Fright Night Film Festival		●								
Frightening Fun		●	●	●	●	●	●			
Frighteningly Funny		●								
Frightfully Fun Frills		●								
Fringe Benefits	●	●	●	●	●	●	●	●	●	
Front & Center						●	●			
Frosty Treats		●		●		●	●	●		
Frou Frou	●									
Fruit Of Labor				●						

	Art & Magic	Fall & Winter	Entertainment	Food	Outings	Reminiscence & Relationships	Sensory	Spring & Summer	Wellness/Health/Beauty	Marketing
Fruits Of Harvest		●		●	●	●	●	●		
Fun & Fab	●			●	●	●	●	●		
Fun Factor		●			●				●	
Fun House		●	●		●	●	●			
Future Self									●	
Games People Play			●							
Gang Of Pumpkins Will Bewitch The Night		●	●	●	●	●				
Garden Debut								●		
Garden Fresh				●				●		
Garden Party					●					
Gather Around The Table With Those You Love						●				
Gathering Place		●			●	●		●		
Gear Up For Some Sooth Summer Driving					●	●	●			
Generations Upon Generations	●	●	●	●	●	●	●	●	●	
Gentle Start To Your Morning					●	●	●		●	
Get A Leg Up									●	
Get Going			●		●	●	●		●	
Get Happy									●	
Get Involved			●	●	●	●	●		●	
Get The Ball Rolling					●					
Get The Picture	●									
Get The Skinny				●					●	
Get The Style You Desire					●			●	●	
Get With The Plan				●	●				●	
Get Wrapped Up In The Holiday		●								

	Art & Magic	Fall & Winter	Entertainment	Food	Outings	Reminiscence & Relationships	Sensory	Spring & Summer	Wellness/Health/Beauty	Marketing
Get Your Bluegrass On			●							
Get Your Style Back									●	
Getting Back On Track									●	
Getting Personal	●			●		●	●		●	
Getting Saucy			●	●		●	●		●	
Getting Started			●	●	●	●	●		●	
Getting The Goods		●	●		●					
Getting There		●			●				●	
Getting To Your Good Place									●	●
Ghoulish Gatherings		●								
Giddy Up			●			●				
Gift Of Good Taste				●		●	●		●	●
Giggling Infectiously			●			●	●		●	
Giggling Is Great						●				
Gilded Accents		●								
Give Me A Field Where The Unmowed Grass Grows					●					
Give Me Liberty			●		●	●		●		
Give Old Things New Uses	●			●						
Glad Tidings		●								
Glad You Asked			●			●	●			
Glamour To Go									●	
Gleam	●									
Glints, Gleams	●	●				●	●			
Glitzy		●	●			●	●			
Global Glamour									●	

	Art & Magic	Fall & Winter	Entertainment	Food	Outings	Reminiscence & Relationships	Sensory	Spring & Summer	Wellness/Health/Beauty	Marketing
Glories Of Autumn		●								
Glowing		●				●	●			
Glowing Orbs		●								
Glows With Warm Welcome		●	●	●		●	●			
Go Ahead Splurge				●						
Go Beyond The Ordinary			●	●	●	●			●	
Go Figure!									●	
Go For The Glow		●				●	●		●	
Go For The Gold		●	●	●	●	●				●
Go The Extra Nautical Mile						●		●	●	
Goddess										
Going Crackers				●			●			
Going Nuts				●			●		●	
Going Nuts For Nutcrackers	●	●	●			●				
Golden Age	●	●	●		●	●	●	●	●	
Golden Moments		●	●		●	●			●	●
Good & Easy				●	●	●	●	●	●	
Good Deal		●			●	●			●	●
Good Deed, Good Fun, Good Read		●			●	●	●		●	
Good Reads		●				●	●			
Good Standard	●					●				
Gooey Goodness				●						
Goose Bumps		●								
Gotta Love....	●	●	●	●	●	●	●	●	●	
Gourmet In A Moment				●						

	Art & Magic	Fall & Winter	Entertainment	Food	Outings	Reminiscence & Relationships	Sensory	Spring & Summer	Wellness/Health/Beauty	Marketing
Grace Our Tables		●		●		●	●		●	
Graceful, Playful									●	
Gracious Gathering			●							
Grand Slam Getaways					●	●		●		
Granddaddy Good						●				
Grasp Life			●	●	●	●	●		●	
Great Food Served With A Side Of Fun & Relaxation			●	●	●	●				
Great For Gathering			●							
Great Greek Delights				●						
Great Moments In History	●		●		●	●				
Great Multi Taskers						●	●			
Great Pick			●	●	●	●			●	●
Great Quotes From Great Minds	●		●			●			●	
Green W/ Envy						●	●	●	●	
Greening Up								●		
Group Hugs		●				●	●		●	
Guest & Glorious.....		●				●				
Gusto			●	●		●	●	●	●	
Hair Raising How Toooos		●								
Hall Partners					●				●	
Halloween Haunts		●								
Handful Of......	●			●		●	●		●	
Handle W/ Care						●				
Hands On Adventure	●		●	●	●	●	●			
Hang Tight						●	●			

	Art & Magic	Fall & Winter	Entertainment	Food	Outings	Reminiscence & Relationships	Sensory	Spring & Summer	Wellness/Health/Beauty	Marketing
Happy Blurred Kaleidoscope Of Time						●				
Happy Days			●							
Happy Feet					●					
Harmony Through Blending	●		●	●	●	●	●		●	
Harrowing Handicrafts (Halloween)		●			●	●	●			
Harvest		●		●	●	●	●			
Harvest Moon		●								
Harvest Scenes		●		●	●	●				
Has Wooded Generations		●			●	●		●		
Hat Happy		●	●		●	●	●	●	●	
Hat Trick		●	●		●	●	●	●	●	
Hats Off						●	●	●	●	
Hats Off To Texas	●	●	●	●	●	●	●	●	●	
Haute Holiday		●								
Have Comfort And Joy		●	●	●		●	●		●	
Have We Got A Story For You						●	●			
Haven					●					
Head Over Heels						●		●	●	
Head To Toe									●	
Heading Outdoors		●			●	●	●	●	●	
Healing Friendships						●			●	
Healing Ritual				●			●		●	
Health Benefits	●	●	●	●	●	●	●	●	●	
Healthy Decadence		●	●	●		●	●		●	
Healthy Gardner					●	●	●	●	●	

	Art & Magic	Fall & Winter	Entertainment	Food	Outings	Reminiscence & Relationships	Sensory	Spring & Summer	Wellness/Health/Beauty	Marketing
Healthy Outdoors A Place To Heal		●			●		●	●	●	
Healthy You									●	
Heart Of The Country					●					
Hearts On Fire						●				
Hearts Sends Warmest Wishes		●				●	●			
Heavenly			●	●	●		●	●		
Heavenly Inspiration	●	●	●	●	●	●	●	●	●	
Hefty				●		●			●	
Help Maintain Health									●	
Helping Hands	●	●	●	●	●	●	●	●	●	●
Hidden Assets		●	●	●		●	●	●	●	
Hidden Joys	●	●	●	●	●	●	●	●		●
Hidden Talent	●	●	●	●	●	●	●	●	●	
Highlights			●	●	●					
Highlights From....	●	●	●	●	●	●	●	●	●	
Highly Dramatic			●		●					
Hip & Historic	●		●			●				
Hip To Be Square						●	●			
Hissy Fit						●				
History Lives	●		●	●		●	●			
Hit The Road					●					
Ho-Hum		●								
Hold Everything						●			●	
Hold The Line										
Holiday Haven		●			●	●		●		

	Art & Magic	Fall & Winter	Entertainment	Food	Outings	Reminiscence & Relationships	Sensory	Spring & Summer	Wellness/Health/Beauty	Marketing
Holiday Merriment		●								
Holiday Money Matters		●								
Holiday Sparklers		●						●		
Holiday Wonderland		●			●					
Homage To Halloween		●								
Home Is Where The Heart Is		●				●	●			●
Homegrown Education	●				●	●	●		●	
Homemade Decisions				●						
Homespun For The Holidays			●							
Homespun Holidays		●				●	●	●		
Honor The Queen..Even If It Is Queen For A Day						●				
Hope Is Blooming		●			●	●	●	●		
Hot Seat			●			●		●		
Hot Stuff				●						●
Hot Topics	●	●	●	●	●	●		●	●	
Hot Trends	●	●	●	●	●	●		●	●	●
How Will You Deal With It?						●				
Hues To Your Health									●	
Humble Squash Turned Into.....		●								
Hungry For Something Special		●	●	●	●	●	●	●		●
I Learned The Hard Way...Now I Trust My Heart						●				
Ice Castles		●								
Ideas For Living Well									●	
If Dreams Could Come True	●					●	●			
If You Carve It They Will Come		●								

	Art & Magic	Fall & Winter	Entertainment	Food	Outings	Reminiscence & Relationships	Sensory	Spring & Summer	Wellness/Health/Beauty	Marketing
If You Dare...		●								
Illuminating Conversation			●							
Illuminating Idea		●								
Illumination	●	●	●			●	●		●	
Illusionary Oasis	●		●			●			●	
Imagine The Endless Possibilities	●	●	●	●	●	●	●		●	
Imagine...Wanting More And Getting It			●	●			●		●	
Immerse Yourself In Good Ole' Times						●	●			
Immerse Yourself In Your Good Times			●		●	●				
Impressive Collection	●		●			●				
Improve Your Smile			●		●	●	●		●	
Improvise					●	●	●			
In A Flash			●	●	●	●	●			
In A Special Light			●							
In A Twinkling		●								
In Honor Of The Harvest		●	●	●	●	●		●		
In The Know	●		●	●	●	●	●		●	
In The Tree Tops								●		
In The Woods		●			●	●	●	●		
In The Zone									●	
Include An Heirloom Tale						●	●			
Incredible Destination					●	●			●	
Indispensable	●		●	●					●	
Indulge Your Passion For....	●		●	●	●	●			●	
Indulge Your Sight	●	●	●	●	●	●	●	●	●	

	Art & Magic	Fall & Winter	Entertainment	Food	Outings	Reminiscence & Relationships	Sensory	Spring & Summer	Wellness/Health/Beauty	Marketing
Infinite Possibilities	●		●	●	●	●	●		●	
Ingenious Solutions			●	●	●	●	●		●	
Initial Reaction	●	●	●	●	●		●	●	●	
Inner Circle			●		●	●	●			
Innovations			●	●	●				●	
Innovations Through The Years	●		●	●	●	●	●		●	
Inside Access										
Insights	●		●	●	●	●	●		●	
Inspirational	●		●				●	●	●	
Inspire Me	●	●	●	●	●	●	●	●	●	
Inspired									●	
Inspired Affection	●					●				
Inspired By		●	●	●	●		●	●	●	
Inspired By Art	●					●	●			
Inspired By Life		●	●	●	●	●	●	●	●	
Inspired By Passion			●							
Inspiring	●									
Instant Style									●	
Interlude			●		●	●				
International Food Tour				●						
Introducing			●	●		●			●	
Introducing Elements Of Nature	●	●			●			●		
Invigorate Your Senses									●	
Invisible Beauty				●		●			●	
Island Attraction			●	●	●	●	●	●		

	Art & Magic	Fall & Winter	Entertainment	Food	Outings	Reminiscence & Relationships	Sensory	Spring & Summer	Wellness/Health/Beauty	Marketing
It Will Make A Memory			●							
It's A Cinch			●	●	●	●			●	
It's A Miracle						●			●	
It's A Wrap			●	●		●	●			
It's All About You						●	●		●	
It's Easy To Join... Just Come	●		●	●	●				●	
It's Your Move	●	●	●	●	●	●	●	●	●	●
It's Your Turn To Talk						●	●		●	
Jagged	●	●				●	●	●		
Jazz Up			●							
Jazzy			●		●	●	●			
Jewel Of A Home	●									
Join Hands And Connect						●				
Journey Back	●	●	●	●	●	●	●	●	●	●
Journey Back In Time			●		●					
Journey Of A Lifetime						●	●			
Joyful Ideas		●								
Joyfulness			●			●	●		●	
July 4th Flourish				●	●			●		
Jump In			●		●	●			●	
Jumping Through Hoops			●			●			●	
Jumpy Vitality						●		●	●	
Junk Gypsies					●	●				
Just A Note						●	●			
Just A Taste				●						

	Art & Magic	Fall & Winter	Entertainment	Food	Outings	Reminiscence & Relationships	Sensory	Spring & Summer	Wellness/Health/Beauty	Marketing
Just Plain Fun	●	●	●	●	●	●	●	●	●	
Just Take It In	●									
Keep Discovering	●		●		●	●			●	
Keep It Real	●		●	●	●	●				
Keep It Sweet						●				
Keep Your Cool						●	●	●	●	
Keep Yourself Open & Alive						●				
Keeping Things Spicy				●						
Key Elements	●									
Key Participants			●			●	●			
Kindred Spirits			●			●	●		●	
Kit And Caboodle			●	●						
Lady Luck			●			●				
Lantern Parade		●								
Last Bite				●						
Last Golden Rays Of Sun		●			●	●	●			
Lasting Value	●					●			●	
Lazy Little River					●	●		●	●	
Leap, Twirl & Soar			●							
Learn Something About People Who Speak In Narrative						●				
Legendary			●			●	●			
Legends Tell Of A Rare......			●			●			●	
Leisurely Float					●	●	●	●	●	
Let It Go									●	
Let It Inspire You			●							

	Art & Magic	Fall & Winter	Entertainment	Food	Outings	Reminiscence & Relationships	Sensory	Spring & Summer	Wellness/Health/Beauty	Marketing
Let's Get Moving									●	
Let's Make A Deal			●			●	●			●
Letter Perfect					●	●			●	
Letting Go			●	●	●				●	
Level Best					●				●	
Life	●	●	●	●	●	●	●	●	●	
Life 101						●				
Life At Home	●	●	●	●		●	●	●	●	●
Life Happens In A Blink						●	●		●	
Life Has A Rhythm						●	●		●	
Life On The Wild Side			●		●					
Life Well Spent						●	●			
Light The Way						●	●	●		
Light Up The Room			●		●	●	●			
Lighten Things Up									●	
Lighten Up			●	●			●	●	●	
Lights Playing	●	●	●		●	●	●	●		
Like A Star		●	●							
Lip Smacking Librations				●		●	●			
Listen & Change Everything						●				
Little Pretties....		●								
Little Sophisticate			●		●					
Live & Learn	●		●	●	●	●	●		●	
Live A Good Life			●	●	●	●	●		●	
Live The Life You Want									●	

	Art & Magic	Fall & Winter	Entertainment	Food	Outings	Reminiscence & Relationships	Sensory	Spring & Summer	Wellness/Health/Beauty	Marketing
Live The Sparkling Life									●	●
Live Well				●					●	
Live Your Life									●	
Lives & Breathes			●				●		●	
Living Artfully	●						●		●	
Living History			●	●	●	●				
Living Large	●	●	●	●	●	●	●	●	●	
Living The Dream	●	●	●	●	●	●	●	●	●	
Local Flavor		●	●	●	●	●	●	●		
Lodge Log Living					●	●				
Long Pauses & Funny Voices						●				
Look For It	●	●	●	●	●	●	●	●	●	
Look Good ..Feel Great									●	
Look Past The Trees	●									
Look What I Found				●	●	●	●		●	
Looking For Some Action			●	●	●	●	●		●	
Looking Glass						●	●		●	
Lovely Gesture						●	●		●	
Loyal	●		●			●			●	
Loyal To						●	●			
Lucky Lunch			●							
Lullaby						●	●			
Lush And Inviting		●		●	●	●	●	●		
Lush Landscapes					●					
Luxurious	●		●	●	●	●	●		●	

	Art & Magic	Fall & Winter	Entertainment	Food	Outings	Reminiscence & Relationships	Sensory	Spring & Summer	Wellness/Health/Beauty	Marketing
Luxury Finish	●									
Luxury...Necessity...Or Both?				●	●	●	●		●	
Made In America				●						
Made In The Shade				●						
Magic	●	●	●	●	●	●	●	●	●	
Magic Match	●					●	●		●	
Make A Statement	●					●			●	●
Make A Statement Without Saying A Word	●						●		●	
Make An Appearance									●	
Make It A Part Of Your Lifestyle	●	●	●	●	●	●	●	●	●	
Make It Happen									●	
Make It Personal	●									
Make It Your Own										●
Make Merry W/ Fantastic Food Fun		●								
Make Our Garden Come To Life		●		●	●	●		●		
Make Summer Come Alive								●		
Make Time For....	●	●	●	●	●	●	●	●	●	
Makes A Statement	●									
Making It Personal	●					●	●		●	
Making Memories		●								
Making The Most Of Everyday									●	●
Manners & Morals									●	
Market Place		●		●	●			●	●	
Marveling	●	●	●	●	●	●		●		
Massive	●		●	●						

	Art & Magic	Fall & Winter	Entertainment	Food	Outings	Reminiscence & Relationships	Sensory	Spring & Summer	Wellness/Health/Beauty	Marketing
Master	●									
Master Your Menu				●						
Matriarchs						●				
Matters Of Taste				●		●	●			
Maximum Merriment			●	●	●	●				
Maximum Potential									●	
Meander					●					
Melodic Journey			●		●	●	●			
Memorable Trip					●	●	●			
Memories	●	●	●	●	●	●	●	●	●	
Memories Are Made In.....						●	●		●	
Memory Makers			●							
Men Will Be Boys			●			●				
Merry & Bright		●	●			●	●		●	
Merry Mayhem			●							
Merry-Go-Round					●	●			●	
Message In A Bottle						●	●			
Mid Party Boost			●							
Midas Touches	●	●	●	●	●	●	●	●		
Midnight Clear		●								
Midnight Snack				●						
Mirth		●								
Mix & Match				●			●			
Mix It Up	●	●	●	●			●	●	●	
Mix Old And New	●		●			●			●	

	Art & Magic	Fall & Winter	Entertainment	Food	Outings	Reminiscence & Relationships	Sensory	Spring & Summer	Wellness/Health/Beauty	Marketing
Modern Twist	●		●	●	●		●		●	
Mojo			●							
Mommyisms						●				
Money Matters						●	●			
Monkey See, Monkey Do			●		●	●	●			
Monstrous		●						●		
Mood Darkens With The Sky		●								
Mood Setting Essentials		●								
Moon Struck		●								
More Choices For Life Well Spent										●
More Please				●						
Morning Breaks Gentle			●	●	●	●	●	●		
Morning Glory			●	●	●	●	●	●		
Morning Silhouette						●	●	●		
Most Revered						●	●			
Most Wanted			●	●		●			●	●
Mouth Watering				●						
Music To Your Ears			●				●		●	
Must See Event	●		●		●					
My Country Life		●		●		●	●	●	●	
Narrow Margins									●	
Natural Instincts									●	
Natural Match	●		●			●			●	
Natural Sense										
Natural Sweetness				●		●	●		●	

	Art & Magic	Fall & Winter	Entertainment	Food	Outings	Reminiscence & Relationships	Sensory	Spring & Summer	Wellness/Health/Beauty	Marketing
Nature & History Dictate	●	●	●	●	●	●	●	●	●	
Nature Inspired	●									
Navigation Plans					●					
Near Peak				●						
Neighbor Network					●	●	●		●	
Neutral	●									
Never Miss A Laugh			●			●	●		●	
Never Slumber Party			●							
New Ideas						●				
New Tricks			●							
News Flash	●		●		●	●			●	
Nice Package		●								
Nights On The Town			●		●	●	●			
No Cooking Required				●						
No More Melt Downs									●	
Nose Around					●	●	●			
Not So Basic	●									
Not Your Typical.......	●	●	●	●	●	●		●	●	
Notable In Suggesting	●		●		●	●			●	
Note Worthy						●	●			
Nothing-To-It	●			●					●	
Notice The Difference									●	
Now You're Talking		●				●			●	
Now You're Thinking						●			●	
Number Crunch						●				

	Art & Magic	Fall & Winter	Entertainment	Food	Outings	Reminiscence & Relationships	Sensory	Spring & Summer	Wellness/Health/Beauty	Marketing
Obelisks	●									
Of The Cuff						●	●			
Off Beat			●							
Off To The Races			●	●	●	●			●	
Often And With Verve			●	●		●	●		●	
Oh, So Simple										
Oh, Those Clever....			●	●		●	●		●	
Old & Improved	●		●	●		●	●		●	
Old Glory			●			●		●		
Old Life						●				
Old School Elegance			●	●		●	●		●	
Old World	●		●	●	●	●	●		●	
Old World Designs	●		●	●	●	●	●		●	
On A Whim						●	●		●	
On The Cutting Edge	●		●	●					●	
On The Road Again			●		●					
On The Side				●						
One For All, All For One			●	●	●	●	●		●	
One For The Road				●	●					
One Good Deed						●	●		●	
One Last Burst Of Excitement			●							
One Of The Most Recognizable	●									
One Pot Pleasures				●		●				
One To Move, Two To Bend, Three To Be You Again									●	
One-On-One Time			●	●						

	Art & Magic	Fall & Winter	Entertainment	Food	Outings	Reminiscence & Relationships	Sensory	Spring & Summer	Wellness/Health/Beauty	Marketing
Only One King Of The Jungle			●		●	●				
Open Door Policy					●	●			●	
Open Spaces	●									
Open The Door To Hope									●	
Open Your Sense Of Adventure					●					
Opportunity To Meditate	●						●		●	
Options Are Almost Limitless	●		●	●	●	●	●		●	
Organized And Effortless	●		●			●			●	
Organized Effort	●		●	●	●	●			●	
Original Classics	●		●	●		●	●		●	
Our Mates					●	●	●			
Our Motto						●	●			
Out & About			●	●	●	●				
Out On A Limb								●		
Out On The Road			●	●	●	●	●			
Out The Door	●	●	●	●	●		●	●	●	
Outdoors Can Be Magical With The Right Illusions	●									
Over-The-Top-Ornamentation		●			●					
Paper Airplane And Paper Kites					●	●		●		
Paper Perfect									●	
Path To Perfection									●	
Patroness	●		●			●				
Pay Homage	●	●	●	●	●	●		●	●	
Peace		●				●	●		●	
Peek-A-Boo			●			●	●			

	Art & Magic	Fall & Winter	Entertainment	Food	Outings	Reminiscence & Relationships	Sensory	Spring & Summer	Wellness/Health/Beauty	Marketing
People And Place	●		●	●	●	●			●	
People Shape & Polish Ordinary Events						●				
Pep Up		●	●	●	●	●	●	●	●	
Perfect First Steps	●				●	●	●		●	
Perfectly Balanced				●					●	
Period Settings			●	●	●	●	●			
Perk Up		●	●	●	●	●	●	●	●	
Personal Roadmap For Your Life Journey					●	●			●	
Personal Style						●			●	
Personality Parade						●	●	●	●	
Personally Created To Make Spirits Bright	●	●	●	●		●	●			
Peruse			●	●	●				●	
Pet Stop			●		●	●	●		●	
Pet Tails/Tales						●				
Pets						●				
Phantom	●		●			●				
Photo Finish	●									
Pick One...Just One				●	●	●	●			
Picker-Uppers									●	
Picture Perfect	●								●	
Piece Of History	●		●	●	●	●				
Pin Up Girl			●			●				
Pint Size Paradise						●				
Pit Stop					●				●	
Pizzazz	●	●	●	●	●	●	●	●	●	

	Art & Magic	Fall & Winter	Entertainment	Food	Outings	Reminiscence & Relationships	Sensory	Spring & Summer	Wellness/Health/Beauty	Marketing
Plan Your Trip Now					●					
Planning To Celebrate			●							
Plant It Forward		●						●		
Playful Parcels	●		●			●	●		●	
Playfulness	●	●	●	●	●	●	●	●	●	
Pleasures Of America								●		
Pleasures Of Summer			●	●	●	●	●	●		
Poetry In Motion	●									
Polite Chit Chat						●				
Politeness			●	●	●	●	●		●	
Politeness Project			●							
Pop	●									
Portrait Of America	●		●	●	●	●	●		●	●
Posture Perfect									●	
Potent Potions				●					●	
Power Of A Woman			●	●	●	●	●		●	
Practical Tips					●					
Precious Pumpkin		●								
Preened						●	●		●	
Present Perfect										
Presto	●	●	●	●	●	●	●	●	●	
Pretty, Yet Practical	●					●			●	
Prickly	●	●		●	●		●	●		
Prime Time	●	●	●	●	●	●	●	●	●	●
Primetime Pig Shin		●								

	Art & Magic	Fall & Winter	Entertainment	Food	Outings	Reminiscence & Relationships	Sensory	Spring & Summer	Wellness/Health/Beauty	Marketing
Privileged Views						●	●			
Professional And Personal Favorites	●	●	●	●	●	●	●	●	●	
Pull Back The Curtain & Glimpse......			●			●	●		●	
Pumpkin Alley		●								
Pumpkin Parade		●								
Pumpkin Patch Picnic		●								
Pursue Your Dreams									●	
Put A Smile On			●	●		●	●		●	●
Put A Smile On Your Face				●						
Quality Time For The Family						●	●	●	●	
Queen For A Day			●	●	●	●	●		●	
Quest Fulfilled										
Quick & Easy				●					●	
Quick Tricks		●								
Quiet Elegance									●	
Quiet Retreat						●	●	●		
Quirk	●		●			●	●		●	
Radiating From Within	●									
Rainbow Connection			●			●	●	●	●	
Raising Spirits		●								
Rampant			●	●						
Reach For The Sky		●	●	●	●	●	●	●	●	●
Reaching New Heights	●		●	●		●	●		●	
Read Of The Month						●	●		●	
Ready Made Romance						●				

	Art & Magic	Fall & Winter	Entertainment	Food	Outings	Reminiscence & Relationships	Sensory	Spring & Summer	Wellness/Health/Beauty	Marketing
Ready To Deal			●							
Ready, Set, Relax						●	●		●	
Reason To Smile	●	●	●	●	●	●	●	●	●	
Reason To Smile Extraordinary Events Of Life						●	●			
Recollection Of A Special Gift						●				
Recycled Chic									●	
Redefining	●									
Rediscover						●			●	
Reflects Your Personality	●		●	●		●	●		●	
Refreshed									●	
Relax And Tour					●					
Relaxation Begins With Reliability									●	
Relaxed									●	
Remarkable	●									
Remarkably					●					
Renew						●	●		●	
Respect	●	●	●	●	●	●	●	●	●	
Rest Upon Their Laurels			●						●	
Restaurant Survival Guide				●						
Restoring Our Heritage						●	●			
Retro Grade					●					
Reuse	●								●	
Revel In The Grass And Shaded Splendor		●			●	●	●	●	●	
Rewriting History						●	●			
Rhythm Of The Woods								●		

	Art & Magic	Fall & Winter	Entertainment	Food	Outings	Reminiscence & Relationships	Sensory	Spring & Summer	Wellness/Health/Beauty	Marketing
Rich History	●		●	●		●	●		●	
Rich Neutral Backdrop	●		●	●		●	●	●		
Right Amount Of Warmth To Cool Places						●	●		●	
Right Up Their Alley			●	●	●	●			●	
Ripe For Discovery				●						
Rituals						●				
Road Trips		●		●	●	●	●	●		
Rodeo Roundup			●		●	●				
Role Reversal			●			●			●	
Romance	●		●	●		●	●			
Romance From The Past						●				
Romance Of The Rural Life		●		●	●	●	●	●	●	
Romantic Details						●				
Room For Memories						●				
Room To Roam					●	●	●			
Roped In	●		●			●				
Rosy Outlook								●		
Round Table Discussion						●				
Round Up				●	●			●		
Round Up Of Smart Talk	●		●		●	●	●		●	
Royal Luxury			●	●		●	●		●	
Running Headlong Into....		●						●		
Rush Of Feelings						●	●		●	
Russet		●				●	●			
Rustic Fantasy			●							

	Art & Magic	Fall & Winter	Entertainment	Food	Outings	Reminiscence & Relationships	Sensory	Spring & Summer	Wellness/Health/Beauty	Marketing
Rusty Hues		●								
Safety Is Number 1									●	
Sassy			●		●	●	●			
Saturated							●			
Saturation Point			●	●						
Saucy & Sensational				●						
Saucy, Sensational & So Much Fun			●							
Save The Date			●	●	●					
Savor The Journey			●	●	●	●	●		●	
Savvy Shopping		●								
Savvy Spots		●			●	●	●			
Scare Up Some Fun		●								
Scoop					●	●	●			
Scoops Of Sunshine In Your Hands					●	●	●	●	●	
Scouting		●			●	●	●			
Screeching		●	●			●	●			
Season Of New Beginnings								●		
Seasonal Delights			●							
Secrets Of Savvy						●	●			
Secrets Of The Savory				●						
Seduction By Chocolate				●		●	●			
See The Benefits									●	
See The Big Picture						●				
Seeing Past The Present	●				●	●	●		●	
Seeing Red		●				●				

	Art & Magic	Fall & Winter	Entertainment	Food	Outings	Reminiscence & Relationships	Sensory	Spring & Summer	Wellness/Health/Beauty	Marketing
Seeing Stars		●								
Seen & Heard			●		●	●	●		●	
Send A Little Love						●				
Send Holiday Greetings In Style		●				●	●	●		
Sensational Spa					●	●	●		●	
Sense Of Character			●			●			●	
Sense Of Evolution	●									
Sense Of Tranquility									●	
September In The South		●	●	●	●	●	●			
Serene	●		●			●	●		●	
Serene Comfort						●	●		●	
Serene Scene						●	●		●	
Set Realistic Goals									●	
Set The Scene	●		●	●	●					
Setting New Standards	●	●	●	●	●	●	●	●	●	
Shades Of Autumn		●	●	●	●	●	●			
Shadows Of The Past	●	●	●	●	●	●	●	●	●	
Shaping Our World And History	●		●		●	●				
Share The Best			●							
Share The Bet										●
Share The Magic		●	●	●		●	●			
Share Top Finds	●		●	●	●	●	●			
Share Your Story						●	●			
Sharp	●		●			●	●		●	
She's Gotta Have It				●		●			●	

	Art & Magic	Fall & Winter	Entertainment	Food	Outings	Reminiscence & Relationships	Sensory	Spring & Summer	Wellness/Health/Beauty	Marketing
Shear Genius						●	●		●	
Sheds Light On Inspiration	●									
Sheds New Light On....			●		●	●	●		●	
Shell Seekers					●	●	●	●	●	
Shine On	●	●	●		●	●	●	●	●	
Shinning Moment		●								
Shock Value	●									
Shoot The Breeze			●		●	●	●		●	
Shopping Connection		●	●	●	●	●				
Show Me			●		●	●	●		●	
Show Your Stripes			●	●	●	●	●	●		
Showering Us With....								●		
Showstoppers	●		●	●						
Side By Side						●				
Side Step			●							
Sidewalk Style					●					
Sign Of The Zodiac			●			●	●			
Signature Drinks				●						
Signature Taste In A Fresh New Way				●	●	●	●		●	
Silhouette	●	●			●			●		
Silk Shimmering Over Your Body							●		●	
Simple Festive			●							
Simple Inspirations						●	●		●	
Simple Pleasures				●						
Simple Pleasures Of The Season	●	●	●	●	●	●	●	●	●	

	Art & Magic	Fall & Winter	Entertainment	Food	Outings	Reminiscence & Relationships	Sensory	Spring & Summer	Wellness/Health/Beauty	Marketing
Simply Exquisite	●	●	●	●	●	●	●	●	●	●
Simply Festive			●							
Simply The Best			●							
Sinister		●					●		●	
Sink In								●		
Sitting Pretty									●	
Skirt The Issue						●	●			
Slam Dunk			●		●					
Slow Lane, Slow Love					●	●				
Slow Methodical Details						●				
Small Changes..Big Impact	●		●	●					●	
Small Indulgence That Seduces Your Senses				●						
Small Wonders	●	●								
Smile, You're Amazing			●			●			●	
Smooth	●		●	●	●	●	●		●	
Smooth Waters					●	●	●	●	●	
Smorgasbord				●						
Snack Shack				●						
Snap Happy			●							
Snazzy Solution			●							
Snow Job		●				●	●			
So Appealing	●	●	●	●	●	●	●	●	●	
So Much More	●	●	●	●	●	●	●	●	●	
Soak Up								●		
Soar To New Heights			●	●		●	●		●	

	Art & Magic	Fall & Winter	Entertainment	Food	Outings	Reminiscence & Relationships	Sensory	Spring & Summer	Wellness/Health/Beauty	Marketing
Soaring Score			●	●		●				
Socializing Between Friends						●				
Soft Touch	●	●		●		●	●	●	●	
Something Wild	●		●	●	●	●				
Something Wild Best Advice						●	●			
Soothing For Mind And Body		●	●	●		●	●	●	●	
Soothing Style	●		●	●		●	●		●	
Soothing Your Style			●	●		●	●		●	
Sophisticated	●	●	●	●	●	●	●	●	●	
Sophisticated Palate				●						
Sophisticated Sparkle		●	●	●	●	●	●	●	●	
Sought After	●		●	●					●	
Source Of Comfort		●	●	●		●	●	●	●	
Southern Character			●	●		●	●		●	
Southern Comfort			●	●		●	●	●		
Southern Comfort N' Joy		●	●	●	●	●	●			
Southern Harm		●								
Southern Soul		●	●	●	●	●	●			
Southern Soul BBQ				●						
Southern Sweet								●		
Spaces To Spark.......		●	●		●	●		●	●	
Spark The Imagination	●	●	●	●	●	●	●		●	
Sparkle	●	●	●			●	●	●	●	
Sparkle And Flair	●	●	●	●		●	●	●	●	
Sparkle And Glow		●	●	●		●	●	●	●	

	Art & Magic	Fall & Winter	Entertainment	Food	Outings	Reminiscence & Relationships	Sensory	Spring & Summer	Wellness/Health/Beauty	Marketing
Sparkling		●								
Sparkling Ideas To Celebrate The Season			●							
Special Delivery		●			●	●	●			
Special Touché That Make Your Day Complete										●
Special Treatment		●	●		●					
Spice Of Life				●						
Spice Up Your Life	●	●	●	●	●	●	●	●	●	
Spider Venom		●								
Spin A Yarn	●		●			●	●			
Spin It						●	●			
Spinning A Yarn						●	●			
Spirits Of The Night		●	●	●	●	●				
Splendid Surprise		●	●	●		●	●			
Splish Splash								●		
Spooktacular Time		●								
Spooky Touches		●								
Spot On	●		●	●		●	●		●	
Spread The Word			●	●	●				●	●
Springtime								●		
Spruce Up						●	●		●	
Spur Seaside Memories						●	●	●	●	
Stand Out From The Crowd									●	
Stand Tall									●	
Stand Under The Trees								●		
Standards Set The Highest In The Industry			●	●					●	

	Art & Magic	Fall & Winter	Entertainment	Food	Outings	Reminiscence & Relationships	Sensory	Spring & Summer	Wellness/Health/Beauty	Marketing
Star Debut			●	●	●	●	●		●	
Star Spangle Performance			●			●	●			
Starry-Eyed	●	●	●					●	●	
Stars Time		●	●			●	●	●		
Stay Motivated									●	
Steady Diet Of Love				●					●	
Step Into The South					●	●	●			
Step Into The World Of Luxury					●	●	●			●
Step It Up									●	
Step Up A Notch				●				●	●	
Steps To Style						●	●		●	
Stick To It									●	
Sticky Situation						●	●			
Stir Up Some Fun				●						
Stirring Up An Sensation	●		●	●	●	●				
Stop To Shop					●					
Store In Style									●	
Storytelling Festival			●	●	●	●	●			
Straight Laced			●			●			●	
Straight, True, Trusted						●			●	●
Strength In Numbers						●				
Stress Management				●			●		●	
Stretch Your Legs, Open Your Mind					●				●	
Striking Costumes	●		●			●			●	
Striking Effect	●	●	●	●		●	●	●		

	Art & Magic	Fall & Winter	Entertainment	Food	Outings	Reminiscence & Relationships	Sensory	Spring & Summer	Wellness/Health/Beauty	Marketing
Stringing Along		●			●					
Stroll Through Spain				●						
Strong Silent Type			●			●				
Structure	●				●				●	
Strut Their Stuff			●							
Stunning	●	●	●	●	●	●	●	●	●	
Stunning Retreat									●	
Stunning Winter Soiree		●	●	●		●				
Sturdy									●	
Style			●			●	●		●	
Style Confection									●	
Style For The Season			●		●				●	
Style Made Simple									●	
Style Statement									●	
Style With Out Excess									●	
Style...With A Little Edge	●		●		●	●	●		●	
Stylish Confections				●						
Stymied	●								●	
Subtle Simplicity			●							
Sugar Coated Holiday		●	●	●	●	●	●	●		
Sum It Up						●			●	
Summer Escape					●			●		
Summer Frazzles			●	●				●		
Summer Pleasures			●	●			●	●		
Summer Rite								●		

	Art & Magic	Fall & Winter	Entertainment	Food	Outings	Reminiscence & Relationships	Sensory	Spring & Summer	Wellness/Health/Beauty	Marketing
Summer Splash								●		
Summer Up								●		
Summon Up						●			●	
Sumptuous				●					●	
Sun Station					●	●	●	●		
Sun Worshippers								●		
Sunny Side Up					●	●	●	●	●	
Sunsets In An Ever Changing Skyline	●				●	●	●	●		
Sure Bet					●					
Sure Shots			●	●	●	●			●	
Surf & Learn					●	●	●	●		
Surprise Package			●							
Surround Yourself With An Array Of Love And Laughter										●
Swanky						●	●		●	
Sweat Smart							●	●	●	
Sweeping								●		
Sweet & Savory				●						
Sweet Dreams						●			●	●
Sweet Heat						●		●		
Sweet Inspiration			●							
Sweet Sips Of Autumn				●						
Sweet Spot				●						
Sweet Summer						●	●	●		
Sweet Summer Social				●						
Sweet Tooth				●	●	●	●			

	Art & Magic	Fall & Winter	Entertainment	Food	Outings	Reminiscence & Relationships	Sensory	Spring & Summer	Wellness/Health/Beauty	Marketing
Sweet, Salty And Southern				●						
Sweetest Part Of Summer				●	●	●	●	●		
Sweets & Treats			●							
Swingin' Good Times			●		●	●				●
Switch Hit					●	●				
Switch It Up	●									
Swooped			●		●			●		
Symmetry	●	●	●	●	●	●	●	●	●	
Table Talk				●	●	●	●			●
Tackle		●							●	
Ta-Da	●		●			●				
Tailgating Done Right		●								
Tailgating Time				●						
Take A Bit				●			●		●	
Take A Bough		●								
Take A Cue			●							
Take A Glimpse				●	●	●	●	●		
Take A Look Inside		●							●	
Take A Stance							●	●		
Take In The View	●	●			●		●			
Take Note	●					●			●	
Take Solace In Deep Moving Water								●		
Take Two			●	●		●	●		●	
Taking The Long View					●					
Taking The Time					●	●	●		●	

	Art & Magic	Fall & Winter	Entertainment	Food	Outings	Reminiscence & Relationships	Sensory	Spring & Summer	Wellness/Health/Beauty	Marketing
Taking Unnecessary Risks									●	
Talking The Talk			●		●	●			●	
Taming The Beast			●		●	●			●	
Tangible Embodiment	●		●	●		●				
Taste				●						
Taste Buds				●						
Taste Of Red Oak		●			●	●	●			
Taste Of Success						●				
Taste Of Tailgating				●						
Taste Of The South				●	●	●	●			
Taste Of Tradition				●						
Tasty Twist			●	●	●	●	●			
Tea For Two						●				
Teamwork	●		●	●	●	●	●		●	
Tell Of Bygone Glories			●		●	●	●			
Tell The Story	●		●		●	●	●			
Telling A Tale						●	●			
Telltale Signs						●				
Tempting Treats			●	●	●		●			
Tender		●	●	●	●	●	●	●	●	
Tender Loving Care				●		●	●			
Terrific Taste				●	●	●	●		●	
Texas Living	●	●	●	●	●	●	●	●	●	
Textures	●	●		●	●		●	●		
The Adventure Begins Today			●	●	●		●		●	

	Art & Magic	Fall & Winter	Entertainment	Food	Outings	Reminiscence & Relationships	Sensory	Spring & Summer	Wellness/Health/Beauty	Marketing
The Art Of Inspiration	●	●	●	●	●	●	●	●	●	●
The Art Of The Basic	●									
The Art Of...	●									
The Balance Of Relationships						●			●	
The Balance Of Romance						●			●	
The Beginning Of Something Wonderful						●			●	●
The Best Memories Start Here	●	●	●	●	●	●	●	●		
The Best Movers									●	●
The Best Of Both Worlds			●			●	●		●	
The Best Stories Never End			●		●	●			●	
The Blahs	●	●	●	●	●	●	●	●	●	
The Briefing						●			●	
The Briefing						●	●			
The Briefing	●		●	●	●	●	●		●	
The Face Of Kindness			●		●	●	●		●	
The Face Of Love						●	●			
The Face Of Sadness						●	●			
The Face Of Surprise						●	●			
The Finer Things In Life	●		●	●	●				●	●
The Flavors Of Fall		●		●	●	●	●			
The Foodies				●						
The Good Life			●			●			●	●
The Great Escape	●				●	●	●			
The Heart Of Life				●		●	●		●	
The Heart Of Southern Life			●	●	●	●				●

	Art & Magic	Fall & Winter	Entertainment	Food	Outings	Reminiscence & Relationships	Sensory	Spring & Summer	Wellness/Health/Beauty	Marketing
The Moves Are For You										●
The Path To Simplicity									●	
The Perfect Blend	●		●	●	●	●	●		●	
The Perfect Solution									●	●
The Quality You Expect..The Life You Enjoy										●
The Real Deal	●	●	●	●	●	●	●	●	●	
The Resulting Art Is Light Filled	●								●	
The Right Time	●	●	●	●	●	●	●	●	●	●
The Secret Of Being Southern						●	●			
The Secret Of Giving						●			●	
The Secrets Out!						●	●			
The Sillies	●		●	●		●	●			
The Soul Of The South Is It's People..You'll Fit Right In			●	●		●				●
The Style Of Your Life						●	●		●	
The Summer's Bet			●	●	●			●		
The Sweet Life				●				●		●
The Sweetest Life I Know						●				
The Temp. Is Great, The Leaves Are Beginning To Glow		●						●		
The Touch Of Caring						●	●		●	
The Touch Of Gold	●	●	●	●		●	●	●		
The Touch Of Silk	●		●			●	●		●	
The True Magic	●	●	●							●
The Wind Is Whipping							●			
Then & Now						●	●		●	●
There Is Always Something To See Or Do			●		●					

	Art & Magic	Fall & Winter	Entertainment	Food	Outings	Reminiscence & Relationships	Sensory	Spring & Summer	Wellness/Health/Beauty	Marketing
There's One To Suit Every Fancy			●		●					
Things We Love	●	●	●	●	●	●	●	●	●	
Think Before You Write						●			●	
Think Fast			●		●	●	●			
Think Pink			●	●	●	●	●			
Think Small						●	●			
Thirst Quenchers				●		●	●			
This Is The Day					●				●	●
This Is The Day To Remember						●	●		●	
This Land Is Your Land	●				●	●	●	●		
This Season Give The Gift Of Relaxation		●					●	●	●	
This Should Be Interesting	●	●	●	●	●	●	●	●	●	
Those Who Are Easily Shocked ...Should Be Shocked More			●		●	●				
Thrill Of The Hunt		●				●				
Through The Glass					●	●			●	
Tidy Transition			●						●	
Tie The Knot					●	●				
Time After Time			●	●	●	●	●		●	
Time For Tea			●	●	●	●	●			
Time Is Marching On						●			●	●
Time Out		●	●	●	●	●	●	●	●	
Timeless Classic						●	●		●	
Timeless Elegance			●	●		●	●		●	●
Timeless Warmth	●	●	●	●		●	●	●	●	●
Tinkling Fingers			●		●	●	●			

	Art & Magic	Fall & Winter	Entertainment	Food	Outings	Reminiscence & Relationships	Sensory	Spring & Summer	Wellness/Health/Beauty	Marketing
To Dine For				●	●					
To The Rescue						●			●	
To Thine Own Self Be True						●	●		●	
Toastmasters			●	●						
Today's Lifestyle	●	●	●	●	●	●	●	●	●	●
Toe The Line						●			●	
Tools And Tips			●	●		●			●	
Top It!	●		●	●	●	●			●	
Top Picks	●		●	●	●	●	●		●	
Tour The Sights					●					●
Transform	●					●			●	
Translating	●		●		●				●	
Travel In Time					●	●	●			
Treasure Chest					●	●	●		●	●
Treasure Hunters Discover....					●	●	●			
Treasured Gift	●					●	●			●
Treasured Islands					●	●				
Trendsetters	●		●	●		●			●	●
Trendy			●	●	●	●	●		●	
Tres Chic	●		●	●	●	●	●		●	
Tried & True			●	●	●	●				
Trip Back In Time	●	●	●	●	●	●	●	●	●	
True Blue			●	●		●			●	
True Companion						●			●	
True To Tradition		●	●	●	●	●			●	

	Art & Magic	Fall & Winter	Entertainment	Food	Outings	Reminiscence & Relationships	Sensory	Spring & Summer	Wellness/Health/Beauty	Marketing
Truly Romantic Gesture			●	●	●	●				
Trusted Favorite		●	●	●	●	●			●	
Tucked		●					●		●	
Tumultuous	●	●	●	●		●				
Tune Into Your Environment			●		●				●	
Tweaks			●	●	●				●	
Twinkle	●	●	●	●	●	●	●	●	●	
Twinkle Toes			●			●	●			
Twist & Shout			●						●	
Two Worlds Meet To Create An Experience Like No Other				●	●	●	●			
Typecast	●		●						●	
Ultimate Anti-Boredom Buster	●	●	●	●	●	●	●	●	●	
Unabashedly Opulent	●		●	●	●		●			
Unbeatable Style									●	
Unbridled Passion						●				
Unclog Your Mind						●	●		●	
Underscore		●			●	●		●	●	
Understanding The Risks						●	●		●	
Unforgettable						●	●			
Unforgettable Holiday Gala		●	●	●		●	●	●		
Unique	●	●	●	●	●	●	●	●	●	
Unique Culture	●	●	●	●	●	●	●	●	●	
Unique Itineraries			●		●	●			●	
Unique Perspective	●		●		●	●			●	
Unique Style	●	●	●					●	●	

	Art & Magic	Fall & Winter	Entertainment	Food	Outings	Reminiscence & Relationships	Sensory	Spring & Summer	Wellness/Health/Beauty	Marketing
Uniquely Delectable				●	●	●	●			
Universally	●									
Unleash The Force	●		●			●	●		●	
Unprecedented Exhibition	●				●	●				
Unpredictable	●	●	●	●	●	●		●		
Unravel The Mystery		●				●				
Unwind			●	●	●		●		●	
Up Close View Of History	●				●	●				
Upcoming			●							
Upscale			●							
Urban Pleasure			●	●	●	●				
Use Good Scents				●		●	●	●	●	
Use Your Skills	●									
Utilitarian	●		●	●	●	●	●		●	
Vacation Inspiration		●		●	●	●	●	●		
Value Is The Luxury										●
Variations On A Theme	●	●	●	●	●	●	●	●	●	
Varieties	●		●	●	●		●		●	
Varity	●		●	●	●		●		●	●
Vast Subjects	●	●	●	●	●	●	●	●	●	
Versatile			●	●			●		●	
Vibrant	●	●	●		●			●		
Victorian	●	●	●	●	●	●	●	●	●	
Viewed To Be The Best	●		●			●			●	
Vignette			●	●			●			

	Art & Magic	Fall & Winter	Entertainment	Food	Outings	Reminiscence & Relationships	Sensory	Spring & Summer	Wellness/Health/Beauty	Marketing
Vintage			●		●	●	●		●	
Visions Of Home	●	●	●	●	●	●	●	●	●	
Visual Treat	●	●		●	●		●	●		
Vivacious Personalities			●							
Voice Of Hope	●					●			●	
Volume And Shape	●		●	●						
Wake Up A Bland Life	●	●	●	●	●	●	●	●	●	
Walk This Way			●	●	●			●	●	
Walk Yourself Thin									●	
Warm & Comfortable		●		●		●	●	●		
Warm & Comforting			●	●	●	●	●	●	●	●
Warm & Cozy		●	●	●	●	●	●	●	●	
Warming Your Shoulders						●	●	●	●	
Warmth		●		●	●	●	●	●	●	
Watch The Fire Flies Flicker								●		
Watchful	●	●	●	●	●		●	●	●	
Water Yourself				●				●	●	
Watermelon Roundup				●	●	●	●	●		
We Love It!	●	●	●	●	●	●	●	●	●	
We Love To Share Food, Stories And Advice..Whether You Ask For It Or Not			●			●				●
We'll Color Your World		●		●			●	●	●	
We'll Make You Feel Right At Home			●	●	●				●	●
Weighing In									●	
Welcome Addition			●	●						●
Welcome Comforts Of Harvest		●	●	●		●	●			

	Art & Magic	Fall & Winter	Entertainment	Food	Outings	Reminiscence & Relationships	Sensory	Spring & Summer	Wellness/Health/Beauty	Marketing
Welcome To The Real World	●	●	●	●	●	●	●	●	●	
Well Contained	●	●			●	●	●	●	●	
Well Past Childhood And Your Children's Childhood	●	●	●	●	●	●	●	●	●	
Western Bucks And Spurs					●	●	●			
What A Deal	●		●	●	●				●	●
What A Great Idea!	●	●	●	●	●	●	●	●	●	●
What A Stud!						●	●			
What It Takes To Conquer A Day			●	●		●	●		●	
What Women Want				●						
What You Need To Know	●		●		●	●			●	●
What's Cookin'	●	●	●	●	●	●	●	●	●	
What's Hot Now								●	●	●
What's New			●						●	●
What's New ...What's Next?	●		●		●				●	
What's On Your Horizon			●		●	●			●	●
What's Right For You...Right Now			●	●	●	●			●	●
What's Your Gut Feeling?	●	●	●	●	●	●	●	●	●	
What's Your Story						●	●			
When 2 Become 1						●			●	
When Heat Overwhelms						●		●		
When Life Gives You a Lemon				●		●	●		●	●
Where Only Eagles Dare	●				●	●	●			●
Where Woman Create			●	●		●	●		●	
Whimsical	●	●	●	●	●	●	●	●	●	

	Art & Magic	Fall & Winter	Entertainment	Food	Outings	Reminiscence & Relationships	Sensory	Spring & Summer	Wellness/Health/Beauty	Marketing
Whirlwind Of Life And Agility			●							
Whittle	●		●		●	●	●			
Who Will Make The First Move			●						●	●
Why It Works	●		●	●	●				●	●
Wicked Good Times		●	●			●				
Wickedly		●	●							
Wickedly Witchy		●	●							
Wild & Wonderful	●		●							
Wild Wonders	●	●	●	●	●	●	●	●	●	
Wild, Wild West	●		●	●	●	●	●			
Winery Tableau				●	●	●	●		●	
Wing It	●		●		●	●	●			
Winner Circle	●	●	●	●	●	●	●	●	●	
Winning Hand			●			●	●			●
Winning Hearts			●			●	●		●	
Winter In The North		●		●	●	●	●		●	
Winter Jewels		●	●		●	●	●			
Wise Up			●	●	●	●	●		●	
Wish To Express Ourselves	●					●	●		●	
Word Of Mouth						●	●			
Words From The Wise	●		●			●			●	
Words To Live By	●		●			●			●	
Words To Work By	●					●			●	
Work Inn Progress	●		●						●	

	Art & Magic	Fall & Winter	Entertainment	Food	Outings	Reminiscence & Relationships	Sensory	Spring & Summer	Wellness/Health/Beauty	Marketing
Work Of Art	●			●						
World Class Fun For Everyone	●	●	●	●	●	●	●	●	●	
World Class Fun For The Family	●	●	●	●	●	●	●	●	●	
Worldly Ways				●						
Worth Cheering For	●		●	●	●	●	●		●	
Worth Exploring	●		●	●	●	●	●		●	
Worth Their Salt						●			●	
Wow Them With Details	●		●	●	●	●	●		●	●
Wrap Your Home In Winter Luxury	●	●								
Wrapped In Light	●	●	●			●	●	●	●	
Write On	●		●			●	●		●	
Yankee Ingenuity					●	●	●		●	
Yearn To Be Found Worthy						●			●	
Ying Yang	●		●		●	●	●		●	
You Are Better If Understood						●	●		●	
You Can Experience The Joy	●	●	●	●	●	●	●	●	●	
You Can See The Stars In The Kitchen				●			●			
You Did It!	●		●			●	●		●	
You Make It Possible						●			●	
You Were Born Ready	●		●	●	●	●	●		●	●
You'll Never Stop Thinking, Creating & Imagining	●					●	●			
You're Not Getting Older You're Getting Smarter						●	●			
You've Got To Forgive						●			●	
Young At Heart						●			●	
Your Attention, Please	●	●	●	●	●	●	●	●	●	

	Art & Magic	Fall & Winter	Entertainment	Food	Outings	Reminiscence & Relationships	Sensory	Spring & Summer	Wellness/Health/Beauty	Marketing
Your Circle Of Friends Just Got A Whole Lot Bigger										●
Your Cup Will Always Be Half Full						●	●		●	
Your Heart's Desire			●			●				
Your Skin Is Million Of Sensors That Let You Feel Your World						●	●		●	
Your Unique Style	●		●	●		●	●		●	
Yum's The Word			●	●	●					
Yummy			●	●	●	●	●		●	
Zest	●		●	●		●	●		●	
Zesty	●	●	●	●	●	●	●	●	●	

Pamela Stoltman has been professionally involved with senior activities for over two decades. Her stomping grounds are in Texas, where she received her undergraduate degrees in Humanities and Theater at the University of Texas at Dallas, and her Masters of Science Social Work (M.S.S.W.), at the University of Texas at Arlington. She is a Nationally Certified Activity Professional (A.D.C.), a Licensed, Certified Assisted Living Director (C.A.L.M.), and a licensed consultant in her field.

Writing with a little tongue-in-cheek, she loves to educate those wanting to learn about her field, and is currently working on a comprehensive book guiding Activity Professionals through the maze of volunteer programs.